HMS Salisbury (1953)

HMS Salisbury seen after her first modernisation, 1961-62. It shows the double-bedstead Type 965P radar on her plated-in mainmast. She still retains her Type 982 aft of the mainmast and a twin 40mm gun which was later replaced by the Sea Cat missile launcher.

(Crown Copyright/MoD)

HMS Plymouth (1959)

HMS Plymouth is seen here prior to her modernisation with original lattice mast and no aviation facilities. There was a single 40mm Bofors on the after superstructure and two triple-barrelled Mk10 Limbó AS mortars in a well deck aft of that.

(Crown Copyright/MoD 1966)

PLYMOUTH

Type 12/Rothesay Class Anti-submarine Frigate

Displacement: 2,600 tons **Dimensions:** 360 ft x 41 ft x 17 ft 3in **Speed:** 30 knots **Complement:** 235 **Armament:** 2 x 4.5-inch (twin mount), 1 x 40mm AA, 2 x Mk10 AS Mortar; 12 x 21-inch AS Torpedo Tubes (four fixed on each beam firing aft and angled at 45°, two twin trainable launchers mounted forward of the fixed tubes, one mounting on each beam). The torpedo tubes were unsuccessful and were removed from all ships by 1963.

Armament following 1966-69 refit: 2 x 4.5-inch (twin mount), Sea Cat missiles (quad launcher), 1 x Mk10 AS Mortar
Aircraft: Wasp helicopter

Laid down: 1 July 1958 **Launched:** 20 July 1959

1961	11 May, commissioned for General Service Commission on Home/East of Suez.
	June, sailed from Devonport as Leader of the 29th Escort Squadron, based at Singapore.
1964-66	Spent 13 months East of Suez.
1966	April. Intercepted the Greek-registered oil tanker *Joanna V* during Beira Patrol.
1966-69	Extensive refit at Chatham. Facilities provided for operating a Wasp helicopter.
1971	Five month refit at Devonport.
1972	July, left Devonport for the West Indies and U.S.A.
1974	Refitted at Gibraltar, under the "Conveyer-belt system."
1975	22 July, left Plymouth for 9 months in Indian Ocean and Far East.
1978	30 May, co-ordinated the destruction of the remains of the Greek tanker *Eleni V* which, 24 days earlier, had been cut in half by a French freighter off the East Anglian coast. 7 September, arrived Chatham for major refit.
1980	October, sea trials.
1981	Captain Sixth Frigate Squadron.
1982	April, exercise Springtrain at Gibraltar. To South Atlantic as part of Task Force to retake Falkland Islands.
1983	Deployed to West Indies and USA until August.
1984	20 January, to West Indies as Senior Ship of the Dartmouth Training Squadron. Returned to UK in April.
1985	April, deployed to Caribbean as West Indies Guard Ship.
	July, refit at Rosyth. Cheverton Motor Boat removed and additional 20mm guns mounted.
1986	Boiler room fire killed two crew.
1987	November, West Indies deployment.
1988	28 April, decommissioned
	Opened to the public for one year at Millbay Dock, Plymouth.
1990	June, bought by the Warship Preservation Trust and towed to Glasgow for public display.
1991	To Cammell Lairds for brief repairs before being placed on public display at Birkenhead.
2006	6 February, Warship Preservation Trust closed citing financial difficulties.
2014	20 August, towed from Birkenhead for recycling in Turkey.

TARTAR

Type 81/Tribal Class General Purpose Frigate

Displacement: 2,300 tons **Dimensions:** 350 ft x 42 ft 3 in x 17 ft 6 in **Speed:** 28 knots **Complement:** 275 **Armament:** 2 x 4.5-inch (single mountings), 2 x 40mm (later replaced by 2 x quad Sea Cat missile launchers), 1 x Mk10 AS Mortar **Aircraft:** Wasp helicopter.

Laid down: 22 October 1959 **Launched:** 19 September 1960

1964	August, returned to Devonport for refit at end of first commission.
1965	Trials and work-up at Portland.
1971	22 November, returned to Devonport, having visited 40 ports in 30 different countries.
1972-73	Refit at Portsmouth. Fitted with Sea Cat guided missiles and improvements to machinery, communications and habitability.
1974	August, deployed to the West Indies, including visits to USA, Bermuda and Caicos Islands.
1975	28 February, gave demonstration of weapon firing and other evolutions to Mexican officials embarked in the Royal Yacht *Britannia* during Her Majesty's State Visit to Mexico. June, in Home Waters.
1975	At the end of the year, she was employed on Fishery Protection duties in the Barents Sea.
1980	March, arrived Chatham to join the Standby Squadron.
1981	August, placed on Disposal list.
1982	17 July, Recommissioned at Devonport having been returned to service to cover for vessels lost and damaged in the Falklands. December, deployed to the West Indies as guardship.
1983	26 June, used explosives to sink 500 ton vessel *Spearfish* that had collided with drilling rig in the English Channel.
1984	29 March, decommissioned at Portsmouth.
1986	3 April, following refit at VT, Woolston, commissioned into Indonesian Navy as *KRI Hasanuddin*.

HMS Tartar (1960)

Her machinery was of a novel design in that it combined steam and gas turbines. The latter's rapid starting properties enabled the ship to leave harbour at short notice; and it boosted the steam turbine when high speed was required.

(Crown Copyright/MoD)

HMS Cleopatra (1964)

As completed the Leander class were well proportioned ships. Armament comprised a twin 4.5-inch turret forward, a quadruple Sea Cat launcher on the hangar roof and a Mk10 Limbo AS mortar in a well aft of the small flight deck.

(Crown Copyright/MoD)

CLEOPATRA

Leander Class General Purpose Frigate (Batch 2A)

Displacement: 2,450 tons **Dimensions:** 360 ft x 43 ft x 18 ft **Speed:** 30 knots **Complement:** 262 **Armament:** 2 x 4.5-inch (twin mount), Sea Cat missiles (quad launcher), 2 x 20mm, 1 x Mk10 AS Mortar **Aircraft:** Wasp helicopter

Armament following conversion: 4 x Exocet MM38 missiles, Sea Cat missiles (3 x quad launcher - 1 forward and 2 on hangar roof), 2 x 40mm AA, 6 x ASW Torpedo Tubes (2 x triple mounts) **Aircraft:** Lynx helicopter

Laid down: 19 June 1963 **Launched:** 25 March 1964

1966	1 March, first commissioned for the Far East.
1967	Spent some months with the Portland Squadron as a Training Ship.
1968-69	Far East Station; over Christmas she was employed on the Beira patrol. Returned to Devonport in October, 1969.
1969-70	From November to March she was employed on exercises, trials and training in Home Waters.
1970	May-September, refit at Devonport.
1972	Escort to HM the Queen and HRH the Duke of Edinburgh visiting Singapore.
1973	Carried out patrols in the Cod War off Iceland with *Scylla*.
1973-75	Extensive modernisation at Devonport - the first Leander class frigate to be fitted with the French Exocet anti-ship surface-to-surface guided missile system.
1975	28 November, recommissioned; during trials she deployed to the Bahamas, Florida and Bermuda.
1977	June, attended Silver Jubilee Review of the Fleet. September 1977 - April 1978, task Group Six deployment to Far East and Australia with *Tiger*, *Amazon*, *Mohawk*, *Rhyl* and *Dreadnought*, supported by *RFAs Tidepool*, *Grey Rover*, *Regent* and *Tarbatness*.
1978	Refit at Devonport.
1979	April, recommissioned.
1980	September, suffered damage to her deck and starboard side during manoeuvres.
1981	Deployed to the Mediterranean in wake of Russian invasion of Afghanistan.
1982	January, entered refit to receive Type 2031 Towed Array.
1983	June, emerged from refit .
1986	July, New York August, Norfolk, Virginia.
1987-89	Major refit at Devonport.
1990	Conducted Exocet missile trials against Goalkeeper off coast of California.
1991	21 August to 11 October, NATO Exercise North Star in North Atlantic.
1992	1 June, decommissioned.
1994	Sold to Cross Seas Shipping Ltd. Beached at Alang, India on 31 January for breaking up.

DANAE

Leander Class General Purpose Frigate

Displacement: 2,450 tons **Dimensions:** 360 ft x 43 ft x 18 ft **Speed:** 28 knots **Complement:** 263 **Armament:** 2 x 4.5-inch (twin mount), Sea Cat missiles (quad launcher), 2 x 20mm, 1 x Mk10 AS Mortar **Aircraft:** Wasp helicopter

Armament following conversion: 4 x Exocet MM38 missiles, Sea Cat missiles (3 x quad launcher - 1 forward and 2 on hangar roof), 2 x 40mm AA, 6 x ASW Torpedo Tubes (2 x triple mounts) **Aircraft:** Lynx helicopter

Laid down: 16 December 1964 **Launched:** 21 October 1965

1967	10 October, first commissioned for trials and work-up at Portland.
1968	19 October, sailed to accompany H.M. the Queen visiting South America.
	After service on Beira patrol, sailed to the Far East.
1970	19 June, recommissioned at Devonport for General Service Commission of four legs - Home/East of Suez/Home/Med.
1972	Toured Eastern Mediterranean and Black Sea.
1974	Persian Gulf and Australia.
1975	November, took part in NATO's largest maritime exercise of the year - 'Ocean Safari' - in N.E. Atlantic and Norwegian Sea.
1976	Further NATO exercises - 'Safe Pass' in March off east coast of USA and 'Open Gate '76' through Straits of Gibraltar.
1977	23 May, returned to Devonport with Seventh Frigate Squadron after 4 months deployment, including a visit to Rio de Janeiro.
1977	1 August, began a 2 year refit at Devonport including installation of Exocet guided missile system.
1980	13 September, recommissioned; her return to sea was delayed by engineering defects to boilers and main engine bearings.
1983	July, emerged from maintenance period with improved close-range armament: a twin 20mm mount fitted aft and two single B-Marc 20mm guns in lieu of ship's boats.
1989	Twelve week docking period extended to fifteen months after serious corrosion found in steel hull plating, frames and longitudinals surrounding the engine and boiler rooms.
1990	Post refit trials followed by five month deployment to the South Atlantic.
1991	July, sold to Ecuador and renamed *Moran Valverde.*

HMS Danae (1965)

HMS Danae was one of seven Leander class to undergo an Exocet conversion. Her 4.5-inch turret has been replaced by four missile canisters for the Exocet anti-ship missile. The Sea Cat capability has been increased by the addition of two further quad launchers and the Limbo mortar removed to provide a larger flightdeck permitting Lynx helicopter operations. Triple ASW torpedo tubes have been added either side of the hangar.

(Syd Goodman Collection)

SCYLLA

Leander Class General Purpose Frigate

Displacement: 2,450 tons **Dimensions:** 360 ft x 43 ft x 18 ft **Speed:** 28 knots **Complement:** 263 **Armament:** 2 x 4.5-inch (twin mount), Sea Cat missiles (quad launcher), 2 x 20mm, 1 x Mk10 AS Mortar **Aircraft:** Wasp helicopter

Armament following conversion: 4 x Exocet MM38 missiles, Sea Wolf missiles (1 x sextuple launcher), 2 x 20mm AA, 6 x ASW Torpedo Tubes (2 x triple mounts) **Aircraft:** Lynx helicopter

Laid down: 17 May 1967 **Launched:** 8 August 1968

1969	16 December, completed for trials.
1970	October-November, off Gibraltar for four weeks of trials - towing the *Penelope* to measure hull noise through the water.
1971	Visited Japan for the annual 'Will Adams Festival' - Adams being credited with the foundation of the Japanese shipbuilding industry.
1972	At Devonport for refit.
1973	22 January, collided with the Torpoint ferry.
	May, in the Cod War off Iceland.
	7 June, deliberately rammed by the Icelandic gunboat *Aegir*, but suffered only superficial damage.
1974	8 March, joint exercise with the U.S.N, and Imperial Iranian Navy in southern Persian Gulf.
	24 June, visited Possession Island, east coast of Australia to commemorate the original ceremony when Lieutenant James Cook landed from *HMS Endeavour* to take possession of the Island 200 years before.
	August, took part in combined exercises off east coast of Malaysia.
1975	1 July, demonstration to Senior Officers and guests of replenishment-at-sea evolutions off Portsmouth.
	4 September, visited Gothenburg, Sweden, when the King of Sweden unveiled a commemorative plaque to the 19th century Admiral, Sir James Saumarez.
1975-76	Further patrols off Iceland in the Cod War.
1976	March, at Devonport presented with the Sopwith Trophy, her ship's flight adjudged the most efficient in 1975.
	25 May, left Plymouth for short spell on Royal escort duties, then to Gibraltar for refit.
1980	August, landed relief parties in the Island of Cayman Brae south of Cuba, which had been devastated by a hurricane.
	November, taken in hand for major refit and conversion for Sea Wolf missile system.
1984	December, completed conversion refit which had been delayed due to manpower being diverted to 1982 Falklands War tasks.
1993	Deployed to South Atlantic.
	December, decommissioned.
2004	27 March, sunk off Whitsand Bay, Cornwall to form an artificial reef; the first of its kind in Europe.

HMS Scylla (1968)

The Sea Wolf conversion required a lot of topweight to be removed from the original ship. The mainmast was replaced by a simple pole mast, the funnel cap was removed and the aft superstructure made much simpler. The Exocet missiles were lowered to the main deck and the port quarter cut away.

(Crown Copyright/MoD)

CRYSTAL

Research and Development Vessel

Displacement: 3,040 tons **Dimensions**: 413 ft 6 in x 56 ft x 5 ft 6 in **Speed:** non-powered **Complement:** 60

Laid Down: 22 June 1970 **Launched:** 22 March 1971

1971	20 March, named. launch delayed by two days due to high winds.
	September, completed.
	30 November, commissioned.
	13 December, towed to Portland.
1975	15 December, towed to Devonport for 6 month refit.
1981	Further refit at Devonport.
1992	18 September, sold to Dutch concern and towed to Rotterdam.

RDV Crystal (1971)

Although not a warship, *RDV Crystal* was the last MoD vessel of significant size to be built and launched at Devonport. She is seen here on her launch day (left) and being manoeuvred in the Hamoaze (above) shortly after entering the water.

(Syd Goodman Collection)

INDEX

A

Aberdeen (1936) 155
Ace (1945) 181
Achates (1945) 181
Adventure (1924) 126
Aeolus (1891) 57
Africa (1862) 7
Algerine (1895) 72
Amethyst (1873) 14
Antelope (1893) 62
Apollo (1934) 153
Arrogant (1896) 75
Astraea (1893) 58
Astrea (1861) 7
Aurora (1913) 108

B

Bideford (1931) 138
Birmingham (1936) 159
Bittern (1861) 8
Bonaventure (1892) 61
Bramble (1938) 167
Britomart (1938) 167
Bulwark (1899) 84

C

Carol (1913) 108
Carron (1867) 9
Centurion (1911) 104, 171
Cleopatra (1915) 114
Cleopatra (1964) 189
Collingwood (1908) 99
Condor (1876) 19
Cornwall (1926) 129
Curlew (1885) 38
Crystal (1970) 195
Cynthia (1861) 8

D

Danae (1965) 190
Devonshire (1927) 130
Dragon (1878) 22
Dryad (1866) 9

E

Edgar (1890) 54
Encounter (1902) 88
Espiegle (1880) 25
Exeter (1929) 133

F

Falmouth (1932) 142
Ferol (1914) 113
Flamingo (1876) 18
Fleetwood (1936) 156
Flirt (1867) 10
Fly (1867) 11
Fowey (1930) 137
Frobisher (1920) 122
Furious (1896) 76

G

Gloucester (1937) 163
Grimsby (1933) 149

H

Halcyon (1894) 66
Harrier (1894) 65
Hastings (1930) 137
Hebe (1936) 160
Hermione (1893) 63
Heroine (1861) 25
Hibernia (1905) 92
Hussar (1894) 69
Hyacinth (1881) 27

I

Icarus (1885) 37
Implacable (1899) 83
Indefatigable (1909) 100

J

J5 (1915) 117
J6 (1915) 117
J7 (1917) 121

K

K6 (1916) 118

K7 (1916) 118
King Edward VII (1903) 91

L

Landrail (1886) 41
Lapwing (1867) 10
Lapwing (1889) 49
Leander (1931) 141
Leda (1937) 163
Leith (1933) 149
Lion (1910) 103
Londonderry (1935) 155
Lowestoft (1934) 150

M

Mariner (1884) 33
Marlborough (1912) 107
Milford (1932) 142
Minotaur (1906) 95
Miranda (1879) 23
Modeste (1873) 17
Montagu (1901) 84
Moorfire (1941) 168
Mutine (1880) 23

N

Nassa (1922)
Northumberland (1928) 130

O

Ocean (1863) 8
Ocean (1898) 79
Olna (1921) 125

Orion (1932) 146

P

Partridge (1888) 45
Pegasus (1878) 22
Pelican (1877) 19
Penzance (1930) 134
Perseverance (1875) 18
Pheasant (1888) 44
Philomel (1890) 53
Phoebe (1890) 50
Phoenix (1879) 22
Phoenix (1895) 72
Plymouth (1959) 185
Polyphemus (1943) 178
Psyche (1898) 80

Q

Queen (1902) 87

R

Racer (1884) 34
Racoon (1887) 42
Rapid (1883) 31
Reindeer (1883) 32
Resistance (1914) 114
Ringdove (1889) 50
Royal Oak (1914) 113
Royalist (1861) 7
Royalist (1883) 28

S

Salisbury (1953) 182

Sandfly (1887) 42
Sapphire (1874) 17
Scylla (1968) 193
Seagull (1868) 11
Seagull (1937) 164
Serpent (1887) 41
Sharpshooter (1888) 46
Sharpshooter (1936) 160
Spanker (1889) 47
Speedwell (1889) 49
Spider (1887) 44
Sydney (1948) 179,180

T

Talbot (1895) 70
Tartar (1960) 186
Temeraire (1907) 96
Tenedos (1870) 13
Terrible (1944) 178
Thetis (1781) 14
Thule (1942) 173
Totem (1943) 174
Trinidad (1939) 168
Truncheon (1944) 177
Tudor (1942) 173

V

Vigilant (1871) 13

W

Warspite (1913) 110
Watson (1919) 121
Wellington (1934) 150
Weston (1932) 145

HMS^s "AMETHYST","MODESTE", "DIAMOND"
ENCOUNTER & SAPPHIRE
3RD CLASS CRUISERS. 1970 TONS
BUILT BETWEEN 1870 & 1874.

HMS Amethyst (1873)

The Amethyst class corvettes were the last wooden warships to be built at a Royal Dockyard, *HM Ships Amethyst*, *Modeste* and *Sapphire* at Devonport, *Diamond* and *Encounter* at Sheerness.

(Allan C. Green courtesy of the State Library of Victoria)

HMS Sapphire (1874)

She was the last wooden corvette built for the Royal Navy before the introduction of composite building. The speediest of her class she was the fastest wooden steam vessel ever to fly the White Ensign.

(Allan C. Green courtesy of the State Library of Victoria)

MODESTE

Amethyst Class Wooden Single Screw Corvette

Displacement: 1,970 tons **Dimensions**: 220 ft x 37 ft x 18 ft **Speed:** 13 knots **Complement:** 220 **Armament:** 14 x 64-pdr

Laid Down: 27 November 1871 **Launched:** 23 May 1873

Sister ship to *Amethyst* and *Sapphire*

1874-81	Spent 7 years on China Station, recommissioning at Hong Kong on 11 May, 1877.
1881	30 September, paid off at Sheerness.
1887	25 January, on the Sales List.
	December, purchased by Messrs. H. Castle & Sons, of Charlton.

SAPPHIRE

Amethyst Class Wooden Single Screw Corvette

Displacement: 1,934 tons **Dimensions**: 220 ft x 37 ft x 18 ft **Speed:** 13.6 knots **Complement:** 226 **Armament:** 12 x 64-pdr

Laid Down: 17 June 1873 **Launched:** 24 September 1874

1875-79	In Australian waters.
1879	9 July, paid off at Devonport; refitted and armament renewed.
1883-89	Two commissions in China; recommissioned at Hong Kong on 27 July, 1886.
1889	25 September, paid off at Sheerness, when she hauled down the last sea-going pendant to fly over a British wooden-hulled ship.
1891	October, condemned as unfit for service and placed on the Sales List.
1892	11 August, sold to Mr. Isaac Cohen of London for breaking up.

PERSEVERANCE

Wooden Paddle-Wheel Tug

Displacement: 540 tons **Dimensions:** 130 ft x 22 ft x 9 ft 6 in **Armament:** None

Laid down: 24 November 1873 **Launched:** 19 January 1875

The launching ceremony included, for the first time, the religious service compiled by the Archbishop of Canterbury which the Admiralty approved for all future launchings.

Used mainly for harbour duties at Devonport.

1884	March, attended the launch of *Amphion* at Pembroke.
1885	August, to Falmouth to survey moorings of the Training Ship *Ganges*.
1909	Transferred to Sheerness.
1910	Placed on the Sales List.
1911	27 April, sold to Messrs. Cox and Co., of Falmouth, for breaking up.

FLAMINGO

Condor Class Composite Single Screw Gun Vessel

Displacement: 780 tons **Dimensions:** 157 ft x 29 ft 6 in x 12 ft 9 in **Speed:** 11½ knots **Complement:** 100 **Armament:** 1 x 7-inch, 2 x 64-pdr
(re-armed with 2 x 5-inch in 1886)

Laid Down: 15 December 1875 **Launched:** 13 December 1876

1877-78	In the Mediterranean.
1879-84	N. America and West Indies Station, recommissioning at Bermuda 23 November, 1880.
1884	October, returned to Devonport, paid off into Reserve.
1886	Refitted when the 7-inch gun was replaced by 2 x 5-inch BL guns.
1887-90	South east coast of America.
1892	Reduced to Harbour Service. Fitted as Coal and Water Depot attached to *Defiance* and moored off Wearde at entrance to Lynher River, Plymouth.
1907	Placed on Sales List.
1909	Fitted as Hospital Ship and loaned to, but in 1923 purchased by, the Plymouth Port Sanitary Authority.
1910	22 March, moored in Jennycliff Bay.
1931	4 May, sold for £777 to Messrs. Demellweek and Redding Ltd, who broke her up in Sutton Harbour, Plymouth.

CONDOR

Condor Class Composite Single Screw Gun Vessel

Displacement: 780 tons **Dimensions**: 157 ft x 29 ft 6 in x 12 ft 9 in **Speed:** 11.9 knots **Complement:** 100 **Armament:** 1 x 7-inch, 2 x 64-pdr

Laid Down: 15 December 1875 **Launched:** 28 December 1876

1877	17 July, commissioned for the Mediterranean where she was to spend next 10 years, commissioning at Malta on 20 August, 1880 and 20 December, 1883.
1882	Took part in the Egyptian War; commanded by Lord Charles Beresford she displayed great daring during bombardment of the forts at Alexandria.
1884-85	In the Red Sea; then refit at Malta.
1887	16 August, arrived Plymouth; paid off to Sales List.
1889	August, sold to Messrs. G. Cohen, Sons & Co., of London.

PELICAN

Osprey Class Composite Single Screw Sloop

Displacement: 1,130 tons **Dimensions**: 170 ft x 36 ft x 15 ft 9 in **Speed:** 12.2 knots **Complement:** 140 **Armament:** 2 x 7-inch, 4 x 64-pdr
(re-armed in 1882-83)

Laid Down: 8 March 1875 **Launched:** 26 April 1877

1877-82	On the Pacific Station.
1882-83	Refit at Devonport when she was re-armed with 2 x 6-inch at quarterdeck broadside ports, 4 x 5-inch at the waist broadside ports and 2 x 5-inch chase guns.
1884-88	Again on the Pacific Station.
1889	19 November, commissioned to spend the next 10 years on the West Indies Station, commissioning at Bermuda in 1892 and 1896.
1899	31 January, paid off at Devonport.
1901	22 January, sold to Hudson Bay Company as a supply ship
1918	August, in action with, and believed to have damaged by gunfire, a German submarine. Post-war became a harbour hulk at Sydney, Nova Scotia.
1953	In the Spring, her hulk was scuttled, with full naval honours, off Sydney harbour.

HMS Condor (1876)

Designed by Nathaniel Barnaby, the Royal Navy Director of Naval Construction, her hull was of composite construction; iron keel, frames, stem and stern posts with wooden planking.

(T. Ferrers-Walker Collection)

HMS Pelican (1877)

Launch was delayed because of the disagreement in manufacturing her machinery. She was consequently fitted with engines intended for her sister ship *Cormorant* building at Chatham.

(Allan C. Green courtesy of the State Library of Victoria)

DRAGON

Doterel Class Composite Single Screw Sloop

Displacement: 1,130 tons **Dimensions**: 170 ft x 36 ft x 15 ft 9 in **Speed:** 11½ knots **Complement:** 140 **Armament:** 2 x 7-inch, 4 x 64-pdr

Laid Down: 26 April 1877 **Launched:** 30 May 1878

1879	19 February, first commissioned for service in East Indies.
1882	Took part in the Egyptian War; landed men as part of a Naval Brigade at Suez.
1882-86	Employed in suppression of slavery in the Persian Gulf and off the east coast of Africa.
1887	27 August, paid off at Devonport.
1892	April, surveyed for possible use as Boys' Training Ship but plan never materialised. 11 August, sold to Mr. J. Read, Jnr, of Portsmouth.

PEGASUS

Doterel Class Composite Single Screw Sloop

Displacement: 1,130 tons **Dimensions**: 170 ft x 36 ft x 15 ft 9 in **Speed:** 11½ knots **Complement:** 140 **Armament:** 2 x 7-inch, 4 x 64-pdr

Laid Down: 9 May 1877 **Launched:** 13 June 1878

1879	5 March, commissioned to spend the next 7 years on the China Station. Recommissioned at Hong Kong on 24 February, 1883.
1886	Returned to Devonport.
1891	Placed on the Sales List.
1892	April, surveyed for proposed use, along with *Dragon* as a Boys' Training Ship, but never so used. 11 August, sold to Messrs. G. Cohen, Sons & Co., of London, for breaking up.

PHOENIX

Doterel Class Composite Single Screw Sloop

Displacement: 1,130 tons **Dimensions**: 170 ft x 36 ft x 15 ft 9 in **Speed:** 12 knots **Complement:** 140 **Armament:** 2 x 7-inch, 4 x 64-pdr

Laid Down: 8 July 1878 **Launched:** 16 September 1879

1880	20 April, commissioned, for the first and only time, for North America and West Indies Station.
1882	12 September, wrecked off Cape East, Prince Edward Island, Canada. No loss of life. Commander and Navigating Officer were court martialled, severely reprimanded and dismissed their ship.

MIRANDA

Doterel Class Composite Single Screw Sloop

Displacement: 1,130 tons **Dimensions**: 170 ft x 36 ft x 15 ft 9 in **Speed:** 11 knots **Complement:** 140 **Armament:** 2 x 7-inch, 4 x 64-pdr

Laid Down: 8 July 1878 **Launched:** 30 September 1879

1880	22 July, commissioned for Australian waters.
1883	22 September, recommissioned at Sydney, N.S.W. Later that year visited Samoa to help quell a civil war raging in the Island of Tutuila.
1884	Toured the Norfolk Islands with Governor of N.S.W.
1886	April-July, cruised amongst the Polynesian Islands.
1887	19 February, arrived Plymouth. 15 March, paid off into Reserve.
1889	March, commenced fitting out at Sheerness as a Surveying Vessel. Later decided it was cheaper to convert the Osprey class sloop *Penguin*.
	Miranda moved to Chatham and was placed in Reserve.
1892	Condemned as unfit for further service.
	11 August, sold to Messrs. J. Read & Co., of Portsmouth, who towed her from Chatham on 24 September.

MUTINE

Doterel Class Composite Single Screw Sloop

Displacement: 1,130 tons **Dimensions**: 170 ft x 36 ft x 15 ft 9 in **Speed:** 11.6 knots **Complement:** 140 **Armament:** 2 x 7-inch, 4 x 64-pdr
(re-armed in 1885-86)

Laid Down: 7 June 1879 **Launched:** 20 July 1880

1881-85	On the Pacific Station.
1885-86	Refit at Devonport when her armament was changed to 10 x 5-inch as in *Espiegle*.
1887-91	On the China Station.
1888	Sent to Chin Kiang to suppress a Chinese riot.
1891	6 March, paid off at Devonport.
1895	Reduced to Harbour Service.
1897	As *Espiegle*, she was fitted as a Boom Defence Vessel for Southampton.
1904	Re-named *Azov*.
1920	Discarded and moored in the Hamble River in the custody of a Care & Maintenance Party.
1921	25 August, sold to C.A. Beard, of Upnor, for breaking up.

HMS Miranda (1879)

A member of the Doterel class, these ships were a revised version of the Osprey class, the graceful clipper bow of the earlier class being replaced by a vertical stem and the engines were more powerful.

(Allan C. Green courtesy of the State Library of Victoria)

ESPIEGLE

Doterel Class Composite Single Screw Sloop

Displacement: 1,130 tons **Dimensions**: 170 ft x 36 ft x 15 ft 9 in **Speed:** 11½ knots **Complement:** 140 **Armament:** 2 x 7-inch, 4 x 64-pdr
(re-armed in 1886)

Laid Down: 23 September 1879 **Launched:** 3 August 1880

1881-85	Australian Station.
1886	Armament changed to 10 x 5-inch - two on the forecastle, two on the poop and the other six on broadside carriages.
1887-91	Pacific Station, paying off at Devonport in November, 1891.
1895	Reduced to Harbour Service.
1897	Fitted as a Boom Defence Vessel for Southampton.
1904	March, renamed *Argo*.
1920	Discarded and moored in the Hamble River.
1921	25 August, sold to a Mr. W. Thorpe.

HEROINE

Satellite Class Composite Single Screw Corvette

Displacement: 1,420 tons **Dimensions**: 200 ft x 38 ft x 15 ft 9 in **Speed:** 13 knots **Complement:** 168 **Armament:** 8 x 6-inch BL

Laid Down: 30 August 1880 **Launched:** 3 December 1881

Laid down as a sloop but reclassified as a corvette in 1883. At the end of 1887 again re-classified as a third class cruiser.
This class was fitted with a telescopic funnel.

1882-85	In the Pacific.
1886-89	On China Station, having recommissioned at Hong Kong, 28 July, 1886.
1887	Searched for the missing Japanese cruiser *Unebi* which had left Singapore on 3 December, 1886 and was never heard of again.
1889	26 June, returned to Plymouth and placed on the non-effective list.
1902	25 August, finally sold to J.J. King & Sons, Ltd., of Bristol.

HMS Hyacinth (1881)

The Satellite class of composite sloops was unique in having an internal steel deck over the machinery and magazines for protection.

(Allan C. Green courtesy of the State Library of Victoria)

HYACINTH

Satellite Class Composite Single Screw Corvette

Displacement: 1,420 tons **Dimensions**: 200 ft x 38 ft x 15 ft 9 in **Speed:** 13 knots **Complement:** 168 **Armament:** 8 x 6-inch BL

Laid Down: 30 August 1880 **Launched:** 20 December 1881

Laid down as a sloop but reclassified as a corvette in 1883. At the end of 1887 again re-classified as a third class cruiser.
This class was fitted with a telescopic funnel.

1886-88	On the Pacific Station.
1889-91	On China Station.
1890	For two days in March, she was aground on an unknown reef off Labourn.
	July, whilst at anchor in Shanghai, she was run into by the *SS Palos*.
1892-96	On the Pacific Station.
1896	March, returned to Devonport and paid off into Reserve, awaiting disposal.
1900	She was used in Keyham Yard to assist in raising the new sheer legs being erected on the south side of North Basin.
1902	25 August, sold to J.J. King & Sons, Ltd., of Bristol.

The seven ships of the Satellite class, of which Devonport built four (*Heroine*, *Hyacinth*, *Royalist* and *Rapid*), were designed by Nathaniel Barnaby, the Royal Navy Director of Naval Construction. The hull was of composite construction with iron keel, frames, stem and stern posts covered with wooden planking. This particular class was unique in having an internal steel deck over the machinery and magazines for protection. The Satellite class were designed to patrol the furthest reaches of Britain's extensive maritime empire and as such spent a considerable amount of time away from UK waters.

ROYALIST

Satellite Class Composite Single Screw Corvette

Displacement: 1,420 tons **Dimensions**: 200 ft x 38 ft x 15 ft 9 in **Speed:** 13 knots **Complement:** 171 **Armament:** 8 x 6-inch BL, 4 x MG

Laid Down: 27 April 1881 **Launched:** 7 March 1883

Laid down as a sloop but reclassified as a corvette in 1883. At the end of 1887 again re-classified as a third class cruiser.
This class was fitted with a telescopic funnel.

On completion she was kept in Reserve.

1886	14 April, commissioned for the Cape of Good Hope and West Coast of Africa.
	November, with *Racer* took part in the Niger River expedition.
1888	Relieved by *Curacoa*, she proceeded to Australia to spend the next 11 years; recommissioning at Sydney in 1889, 1893 and 1896.
1899	17 October, arrived Plymouth.
	13 November, sailed to Queenstown to be converted to a hulk for the reception of ships' crews at Haulbowline.
1913	1 December, commissioned as a Receiving Ship at Queenstown and renamed *Colleen*.
1914-19	Wore the Flag of C-in-C Coast of Ireland.
1920-22	Wore the Flag of C-in-C Western Approaches.
1922	15 March, paid off at Haulbowline.
1923	19 February, handed over to the Irish Government, who used her as an oil hulk.
1950	Believed to have been broken up.

HMS Royalist (1883)

Although four of her sister ships were armed with two 6-inch and ten 5-inch breech-loading guns, *Royalist*, in common with *Heroine* and *Hyacinth*, received an outfit of eight BL 6-inch/100-pdr guns, complemented with a light gun and 4 machine guns.

(*T. Ferrers-Walker Collection*)

HMS Rapid (1883)

A report in *The Times* (London) on 10 March 1902 suggested that *HMS Rapid* was to be sold out of service owing to defects in her machinery.

(Allan C. Green courtesy of the State Library of Victoria)

RAPID

Satellite Class Composite Single Screw Corvette

Displacement: 1,420 tons **Dimensions**: 200 ft x 38 ft x 15 ft 9 in **Speed:** 13 knots **Complement:** 171 **Armament:** 2 x 6-inch; 10 x 5-inch

Laid Down: 21 April 1881 **Launched:** 21 March 1883

Changes in classification were as *Heroine*.

At her launching she collided with the *Royal Adelaide*, which was moored 900 yards off, and badly damaged both ships.

1884	9 September, commissioned for the Cape of Good Hope and West Coast of Africa.
1885-86	December - March, refitted at Simon's Bay; then directed to Australian waters.
1888	January, visited New Zealand.
	March, recommissioned at Sydney, N.S.W.
1888-98	Spent 10 years on the Australian Station, recommissioning at Sydney at three-yearly intervals.
1898	Returned to UK. Gale force winds and engine trouble caused a voyage of 4 months instead of the normal 6 weeks.
1902	Placed on the Sales List at Plymouth.
	September, towed by the tug *Energetic* to Gibraltar for use there as an accommodation ship for Dockyard workmen.
1912	Became Submarine Depot Ship at Gibraltar.
1916	Renamed *Hart*.
1948	Sold to a Spanish scrap dealer; towed to Malaga for breaking up.

REINDEER

Mariner Class Composite Single Screw Gun Vessel

Displacement: 970 tons **Dimensions**: 167 ft x 32 ft x 14 ft **Speed:** 12½ knots **Complement:** 126 **Armament:** 6 x 5-inch

(with only 1 gun on the forecastle and one aft, she was the least powerfully armed of the class)

Laid Down: 15 January 1883 **Launched:** 14 November 1883

Re-rated as a sloop on 26 November 1884

1884	4 December, commissioned for the East Indies; after 4 months off Aden and Somali coast, she proceeded to the Persian Gulf.
1886	June, after refit at Trincomalee, she was engaged off Zanzibar in the suppression of slave trade.
1888	23 January, paid off at Bombay.
1888-91	Again engaged in the suppression of slave trade and blockade of the East African coast; captured 9 dhows and freed 140 slaves.
1891	20 February, she was almost wrecked when entering Malta; saved from being driven on to rocks by 'making sail'.
1895	Reduced to Harbour Service at Devonport.
1903	Brought forward for use as a Boom Defence Vessel at Devonport along with *Mariner*.
1917	Converted to a Salvage Vessel.
1919	Taken over by the Liverpool Salvage Association who renamed her *Reindeer 1*. Her last job was with airship R38 which crashed in flames into the Humber.
1924	12 July, sold to Halifax Shipyard Ltd. as a salvage vessel.
1932	March, abandoned at sea off Halifax; her crew was picked up by CPR liner *Montcalm*.

The Mariner class was a class of six 8-gun sloops built for the Royal Navy between 1883 and 1888. Again four were built at Devonport. Also of composite construction they were powered by a 2-cylinder horizontal compound-expansion steam engine driving a single screw. They were also built as barque-rigged vessels.

MARINER

Mariner Class Composite Single Screw Gun Vessel

Displacement: 970 tons **Dimensions**: 167 ft x 32 ft x 14 ft **Speed:** 12 knots **Complement:** 126 **Armament:** 8 x 5-inch
(two each end and two each side amidships)

Laid Down: 8 January 1883 **Launched:** 23 June 1884

Re-rated a sloop on 26 November 1884.

1885	March, commissioned for Particular Service.
	10 June, joined the British Evolutionary Squadron, formed to test the practical efficiency of the 'material' of the Fleet.
	1 September, proceeded to the Mediterranean; then to East Indies.
1889	10 January, recommissioned at Trincomalee; employed in the blockade of the East African coast.
1891-92	On the Cape of Good Hope and West Coast of Africa Station.
1892-95	In Reserve at Devonport before being reduced to Harbour Service.
1903	Along with *Reindeer* became a Boom Defence Vessel at Devonport.
1915	November, taken in hand for conversion to a Salvage Vessel.
1919-21	Under the management of the Liverpool Salvage Association.
1922-29	Laid up at Southampton.
1929	19 February, sold to Hughes Bolckow & Co. Ltd. of Blyth for breaking up.

RACER

Mariner Class Composite Single Screw Gun Vessel

Displacement: 970 tons **Dimensions**: 167 ft x 32 ft x 14 ft **Speed:** 12½ knots **Complement:** 126 **Armament:** 8 x 5-inch
(two each end and two each side amidships)

Laid Down: 9 April 1883 **Launched:** 6 August 1884

Re-rated a sloop on 26 November 1884.

1885	9 April, commissioned for the Cape of Good Hope and West Coast of Africa Station.
	June, joined the British Evolutionary Squadron (see *Mariner*).
	29 August, left Plymouth for the Cape.
1886	October, employed on duties for the Niger River expedition.
1887	27 January, proceeded for 200 miles up the River Gambia. June, joined the Mediterranean Squadron.
	December, ordered east to Sakin in the Sudan.
1889	16 April, returned to Devonport.
	10 May, paid off into Reserve.
1891-92	Again on the Cape of Good Hope and West Coast of Africa Station.
1893-94	South East Coast of America.
1896	After refit, she commissioned as a Tender to *Britannia* at Dartmouth.
1903	February, left Dartmouth for Portsmouth; used as a Tender to Osborne College in the Isle of Wight.
1917	Converted to a Salvage Vessel. She played an important part over several years in salvaging the gold from the White Star liner *Laurentic*, mined and sunk off Ireland when acting as an Armed Merchant Cruiser.
1928	6 November, sold to Hughes Bolckow Ltd., of BIyth, for breaking up.

HMS Racer (1884)

These composite screw gun vessels were very good for providing a presence in overseas territories but their effectiveness as a frontline warship was doubtful.

(*Naval History & Heritage Command NH64218*)

HMS Icarus (1885)

All the ships of the class were built as barque-rigged vessels, except *Icarus*, which had no main yards provided, making her a barquentine.

(Naval History & Heritage Command NH88869)

ICARUS

Mariner Class Composite Single Screw Gun Vessel

Displacement: 970 tons **Dimensions**: 167 ft x 32 ft x 14 ft **Speed:** 12 knots **Complement:** 126 **Armament:** 8 x 5-inch
(two each end and two each side amidships)

Laid Down: 18 August 1883 **Launched:** 27 July 1885

Re-rated a sloop on 26 November 1884.

1886-88	6 July, commissioned for the Cape of Good Hope Station.
1888-90	On the Pacific Station.
1890	May, on her return to Devonport, her Commanding Officer was court martialled and found guilty of having ordered unapproved punishments to ratings.
	July, proceeded to Sheerness for refit, when her armament was increased by the addition of Q.F. guns.
1891-95	In Reserve at Chatham.
1895-1902	On the Pacific Station.
1902	May, paid off at Sheerness.
	September, placed on the Sales List.
1904	12 April, sold for £3,900.

CURLEW

Curlew Class Steel, Twin Screw First Class Gun Vessel

Displacement: 950 tons **Dimensions**: 195 ft x 28 ft x 10 ft 6 in **Speed:** 14½ knots **Complement:** 105 **Armament:** 1 x 6-inch, 3 x 5-inch, 3 x Torpedo Tubes (1 bow, 2 launching carriages)

Laid Down: 5 January 1885 **Launched:** 23 October 1885

1886-92	Channel Squadron.
1892	Replaced *Plucky* as Tender to *Cambridge*, the Gunnery Ship at Devonport.
1902	November, her bow T.T. and bow and stern guns were removed prior to replacing *Jason* on the Irish Station.
1903-04	Coastguard Tender on the Irish Station.
1904	December, paid off at Devonport.
1905	Laid up at Motherbank, Portsmouth.
1906	10 July, sold at Portsmouth for £3,625.

HMS Curlew (1885)

The building of *Curlew* and *Landrail* saw a further development in shipbuilding with mild steel replacing iron. When first tried in 1881 for parts of the hull of the corvette *Heroine*, it raised much doubt, for it frequently occurred that mild steel plates, after being heated and worked into shape and placed into position one day, would on the next morning be found to be seriously fractured, especially after a cold frosty night. The Admiralty, in conjunction with the steel makers, conducted extensive experiments and research. The failure was found to be chiefly due to overheating of the metal and to prevent such failure it was ordered that the metal should not be heated beyond a certain limiting temperature, and that it was essential it be gradually cooled afterwards.

(Naval History & Heritage Command NH88873)

HMS Serpent (1887)

To prevent corrosion of internal plating which was likely to come into contact with water - such as floor plates, lower plating of bulkheads etc - the process of galvanising was adopted. This was first introduced at Devonport during the construction of *Serpent*.

(T. Ferrers-Walker Collection)

LANDRAIL

Curlew Class Steel Twin Screw First Class Gun Vessel

Displacement: 950 tons **Dimensions**: 195 ft x 28 ft x 10 ft 6 in **Speed:** 14½ knots **Complement:** 105 **Armament:** 1 x 6-inch, 3 x 5-inch, 3 x Torpedo Tubes (1 bow, 2 launching carriages)

Laid Down: 5 January 1885 **Launched:** 19 January 1886

1887-89	On the West Coast of Africa.
1889-93	In the Mediterranean Fleet; recommissioning at Malta in 1890.
1893	Commissioned at Sheerness as Tender to the Flagship *Wildfire* for service with the Gunnery School.
1896	11 July, in collision with, and sunk, the barque *Siren* off Portland; she was repaired in dock at Sheerness.
1901-02	Refit at Sheerness; afterwards placed in Fleet Reserve.
1902	October, again refitted, to fit her as a replacement for *Circe*, the Tender to *Severn*, the Coastguard Ship at Harwich.
1903	Employed on Fishery Protection duties.
	2 November, went aground on Egmond Beach, north of Ymuiden; on shore for 9 hours.
1905	June, placed on the Sales List at Sheerness.
1906	Filled with cork and empty barrels, she was used as a target vessel at Portland.
	4 October, whilst being towed back to harbour, she sank without warning. All on board - except one signalman - were picked up.

SERPENT

Archer Class Twin Screw Third Class Cruiser

Displacement: 1,770 tons **Dimensions**: 225 ft x 36 ft x 13 ft 6 in **Speed:** 17 knots **Complement:** 176 **Armament:** 6 x 6-inch, 8 x 3-pdr, 5 x 14-inch Torpedo Tubes (1 bow, 4 broadside). It was intended that she have 10 tubes, but as the designed displacement of 1,600 tons had been exceeded, the number of tubes was halved.

Laid Down: 9 November 1885 **Launched:** 10 March 1887

Her construction saw the introduction of galvanising to bulkhead plating, floor plates, etc., exposed to bilge water.

1888	Commissioned for Annual Manoeuvres, but after 8 weeks was placed in Reserve.
1889	Commissioned for Annual Manoeuvres, then placed in Reserve.
1890	24 June, commissioned for service on the Cape of Good Hope and West Coast of Africa Station.
	8 November, left Plymouth.
	10 November, wrecked when she struck Boy Rock, in Punta Bay, near Cape Villano on north coast of Spain. Only 3 ratings survived. Verdict of the Court of Enquiry was that *Serpent* was lost through an error of navigation.

RACOON

Archer Class Twin Screw Third Class Cruiser

Displacement: 1,770 tons **Dimensions**: 225 ft x 36 ft x 13 ft 6 in **Speed:** 17 knots **Complement:** 176 **Armament:** 6 x 6-inch, 8 x 3-pdr, 5 x 14-inch Torpedo Tubes (as *Serpent*)

Laid Down: 1 February 1886 **Launched:** 6 May 1887

Construction feature as *Serpent*

1889-1891	Reserve at Devonport.
1891	2 April, commissioned for the Cape of Good Hope and West Coast of Africa Station.
1894	3 June, recommissioned at Simon's Bay.
1897	12 August, returned to Sheerness; paid off into Reserve.
	Refitted when her 6-inch B.L. guns were exchanged for 6-inch converted Q.F. guns.
1898	1 February, commissioned for the East Indies.
1901	14 June, returned to Sheerness. After 4 months under repair, her sister ship *Porpoise* was refitted in her stead.
1904	Placed on the Sales List.
1905	4 April, sold at Chatham Dockyard to Messrs. G. Cohen, Sons & Co., of London for £4,150.

SANDFLY

Grasshopper Class Twin Screw First Class Torpedo Gunboat

Displacement: 525 tons **Dimensions**: 200 ft x 23 ft x 9 ft **Speed:** 19 knots **Complement:** 63 **Armament:** 1 x 4-inch, 6 x 3-pdr, 4 x 14-inch Torpedo Tubes (1 bow, 1 stern and one launching carriage each side)

Laid Down: 19 April 1886 **Launched:** 30 September 1887

1890	24 June, commissioned for the Mediterranean.
1894	3 June, paid off at Malta; remaining there for the next 10 years.
1905	17 March, sold for £1,805 for breaking up.

HMS Sandfly (1887)

Originally designed as anti-torpedo boats, known as 'Torpedo Boat Catchers', but proved too slow and were replaced by Torpedo Boat Destroyers. She was a long time on the slipway because of the Admiralty's delay in placing a contract for her machinery.

(*Allan C. Green courtesy of the State Library of Victoria*)

SPIDER

Grasshopper Class Twin Screw First Class Torpedo Gunboat

Displacement: 525 tons **Dimensions**: 200 ft x 23 ft x 9 ft **Speed:** 19 knots **Complement:** 63 **Armament:** 1 x 4-inch, 6 x 3-pdr,
4 x 14-inch Torpedo Tubes (as *Sandfly*)

Laid Down: 7 June 1886 **Launched:** 17 October 1887
She was launched complete with engines.

1892	March, transferred to Dockyard Reserve and placed at the disposal of Engineer Students at Keyham College. 20 April, commissioned as Tender to *Vivid*.
1896	Refitted; engines and boilers being overhauled by the Engineer Students.
1902	Intention to refit her was found to be uneconomic, so in September she was placed on the Sales List.
1903	13 May, sold at auction at Devonport for £1,820 to Messrs. T.W. Ward Ltd., of Sheffield. Condition of the sale was that she had to be broken up in the UK within 1 year.

PHEASANT

Pigmy Class Composite Single Screw First Class Gunboat

Displacement: 755 tons **Dimensions**: 165 ft x 30 ft x 11 ft 3 in **Speed:** 13.2 knots **Complement:** 76 **Armament:** 6 x 4-inch

Laid Down: 6 June 1887 **Launched:** 10 April 1888

The first time, along with the *Partridge*, that engines for a ship of war had been made in the Dockyard.

1888	30 October, commissioned for the Cape of Good Hope and West Coast of Africa Station.
1890	Ordered to the Pacific where she was to remain for the next 10 years. Recommissioned at Esquimault in December, 1891, October, 1894, and October, 1897.
1901	23 April, returned to Plymouth; paid off and transferred to Dockyard to be refitted for further service. However, she was never to recommission.
1906	15 May, sold at Devonport to Messrs. Cox and Co., of Falmouth, for £2,900.

PARTRIDGE

Pigmy Class Composite Single Screw First Class Gunboat.

Displacement: 755 tons
Dimensions: 165 ft x 30 ft x 11 ft 3 in
Speed: 13.2 knots
Complement: 76
Armament: 6 x 4-inch

Laid Down: 6 June 1887 **Launched:** 10 May 1888

Engined by the Dockyard - see *Pheasant*.

1888	12 December, first commissioned.
1889	3 January, collided with, and badly damaged, a Penzance fishing smack, *No.114*.
	20 January, left Plymouth for North America & West Indies Station.
1892	22 March, recommissioned at Bermuda.
1895	5 April, again recommissioned at Bermuda.
1898	29 October, arrived Plymouth; paid off into Reserve. A week later a navigating party took her to Sheerness for refit.
1899	4 May, commissioned at Chatham for the Cape of Good Hope and West Coast of Africa Station, where she was to spend the rest of her days. Recommissioned at Simon's Town in May, 1902.
1904	November, paid off at Simon's Town to the Sales List.
1912	Sold at Simon's Town to T.W. Ward Ltd., of Preston.

HMS Partridge (1888)

(Detroit Publishing Co. courtesy of the Library of Congress)

SHARPSHOOTER

Sharpshooter Class Twin Screw First Class Torpedo Gunboat

Displacement: 735 tons **Dimensions**: 230 ft x 27 ft x 8 ft 3 in **Speed:** 21 knots **Complement:** 91 **Armament:** 2 x 4.7-inch, 4 x 3-pdr, 3 x 14-inch Torpedo Tubes (1 bow and 1 launching carriage on each side)

Laid Down: 13 January 1888 **Launched:** 30 November 1888

Designed as improved *Sandfly* and *Spider* but she proved to be the forerunner of more unsatisfactory, slow steaming Torpedo Boats

1891	Her guns were removed and fitted in the Australian cruiser *Tauranga*.
1892	January, new guns fitted.
1894	Fitted with new Belleville tubulous boilers. Breakdowns were frequent during her trials.
1895-97	Being the first man-of-war fitted with water-tube boilers she was used for instruction in their use, as a sea-going vessel, by the students at Royal Navy Engineering College (RNEC), Keyham.
1904	18 November, to Queenstown as Drill Ship for the RNR.
	24 February, returned to Plymouth to become a Tender to the *Vivid*.
1905	July, after refit at Devonport, she was detailed for duty with Inspecting Captain of Submarines.
1910	July, collided with submarine *B4* off Milford Haven.
1911	September, transferred to Harwich for duty with submarines.
1912	June, paid off at Chatham, and later in the year placed on the Sales List.
1913	March, lent to Lord Northampton as a Boys' Training Ship.
1914	Renamed *Northampton*.
1919	Lent to the Boy Scouts Association, moored off the Thames Embankment.
1922	27 March, sold to C.A. Beard, of Upnor.
	7 April, towed to Upnor, opposite Chatham Dockyard, for breaking up.

SPANKER

Sharpshooter Class Twin Screw First Class Torpedo Gunboat

Displacement: 735 tons **Dimensions**: 230 ft x 27 ft x 8 ft 3 in **Speed:** 21 knots **Complement:** 91 **Armament:** 2 x 4.7-inch, 4 x 3-pdr, 3 x 14-inch Torpedo Tubes (as *Sharpshooter*)

Laid Down: 12 April 1888 **Launched:** 27 February 1889

1890-92	On several occasions she suffered major defects in her boilers.
1893	Fitted with new boilers.
1896	Became a Tender to *Alexandra*, the Coastguard Ship at Portland.
1901	Re-commissioned as Tender to *Revenge* who was then the Coastguard Ship at Portland.
1905-06	In Reserve at Portsmouth.
1907	In the Home Fleet.
1908	8 March, her engines failed when off the Isle of Wight and had to be towed back to Portsmouth. Ran on to a sandbank during the tow; docked on arrival.
1911	December, collided with an Austrian steamer in the Thames Estuary; required repair at Portsmouth.
1914	Converted to a Fleet Minesweeper, attached to the Grand Fleet. August, took part in operations against Zeebrugge.
1917	June, attached to the Grand Fleet.
1918	September, joined gunboats at Oban.
1920	20 March, sold for £3,333 to the Cornish Salvage (1918) Co. Ltd., and broken up at their yard at Ilfracombe.

HMS Speedwell (1889)

The Sharpshooter class was intended for 21 knots but all, except *Seagull*, had the unreliable 'locomotive' boiler which meant that their trial speeds were closer to 19 knots. Later, most were re-boilered and able to achieve 21 knots, though in practice the ships lost speed very rapidly in a seaway.

(Syd Goodman Collection)

SPEEDWELL

Sharpshooter Class Twin Screw First Class Torpedo Gunboat

Displacement: 735 tons **Dimensions**: 230 ft x 27 ft x 8 ft 3 in **Speed:** 21 knots **Complement:** 91 **Armament:** 2 x 4.7-inch, 4 x 3-pdr, 3 x 14-inch Torpedo Tubes (as *Sharpshooter*)

Laid Down: 18 April 1888 **Launched:** 15 March 1889

1890	1 July, first commissioned for the Channel Squadron. During Naval Maneuvres, collided with a merchant ship. Repaired in Devonport Dockyard.
1894	September, paid off into Dockyard Reserve.
1899-1900	Refitted and re-engined at Palmer's Shipyard, Jarrow.
1900	September, commissioned as a Tender to *Rodney*, the Coastguard Ship at Queensferry in Scotland.
1905	November, again placed in Reserve.
1907	With the Home Fleet at the Nore.
1914	Adapted for minesweeping; classed as a Fleet Minesweeper, attached to the Grand Fleet.
1917	January, in the Second Fleet-Sweeping Flotilla.
	June, became ship of the Senior Officer of Gunboats at Oban.
1919	Became Tender to *Colleen*, Receiving Ship at Queenstown.
	At end of year, was placed on the Sales List.
1920	20 March, sold to Cornish Salvage (1918) Co. Ltd., and broken up at their yard at Ilfracombe.

LAPWING

Redbreast Class Composite Single Screw First Class Gunboat

Displacement: 805 tons **Dimensions**: 165 ft x 31 ft x 12 ft 3 in **Speed:** 13 knots **Complement:** 76 **Armament:** 6 x 4-inch, 2 x 3-pdr

Laid Down: 1 May 1888 **Launched:** 12 April 1889

1890	16 September, commissioned to spend the next 10 years in the East Indies. On passage she visited Northern Spain seeking information on the fate of *Serpent*. Salvaged a few items from the wreck.
1900	12 July, arrived Devonport; paid off into Dockyard Reserve.
	18 October, left Devonport for Haulbowline for refit, during which her Q.F. guns were replaced with breech-loaders.
1901	16 May, again sailed for the East Indies, never to return to the UK. Recommissioned on 3 occasions at Bombay.
1910	10 November, sold at Bombay.

RINGDOVE

Redbreast Class Composite Single Screw First Class Gunboat

Displacement: 805 tons **Dimensions**: 165 ft x 31 ft x 12 ft 3 in **Speed:** 13 knots **Complement:** 76 **Armament:** 6 x 4-inch (later reduced to 4), 2 x 3-pdr

Laid Down: 1 June 1888 **Launched:** 30 April 1889

1890	16 September, commissioned for service in Australian waters.
1894	24 February, recommissioned at Sydney, N.S.W.
1897	4 July, returned to Devonport; paid off into Dockyard Reserve for refit.
	9 November, recommissioned for further 4 years in Australian waters.
1901	20 May, returned to Devonport.
	7 June, paid off for refit at Haulbowline, but that yard was so busy, she returned to Devonport; placed in Reserve.
1905	April - September, service with Newfoundland Fisheries.
1906-13	Fishery Protection duties off coast of Scotland.
1916	Renamed *Melita*.
1917	Converted to a Salvage Vessel.
1920	22 January, sold to Ship Salvage Corporation. Believed she was still operating at Falmouth, privately owned, in 1923.

PHOEBE

Pearl Class Twin Screw Third Class Protected Cruiser

Displacement: 2,575 tons **Dimensions**: 265 ft x 41 ft x 15 ft **Speed:** 19 knots **Complement:** 190 **Armament:** 8 x 4.7-inch, 8 x 3-pdr, 4 x 14-inch Torpedo Tubes (1 bow, 1 stern, 2 broadside, all above water)

Laid Down: 23 April 1889 **Launched:** 1 July 1890

1891	25 August, boiler explosion whilst on trials.
1892	1 December, commissioned for the Cape of Good Hope and West Coast of Africa Station.
1894	August - September, took part in operations in the Benin River; landed armed parties.
1896-99	Unhealthy climate on the West Coast wrought havoc amongst her crew. Several died and many invalided home. Only 40 of the original crew came home with the ship.
1899-1901	Extensive refit at Devonport.
1901-05	In Australian waters; recommissioned at Sydney, N.S.W. in November, 1904.
1905	23 December, paid off at Portsmouth; then placed on the Sales List.
1906	10 July, sold at Portsmouth for £9,850 to A. Anderson of Copenhagen.

HMS Phoebe (1890)

One of a class of nine such vessels, five of which were paid for by Australia, under the terms of the Imperial Defence Act of 1887, to serve in Australian waters.

(Allan C. Green courtesy of the State Library of Victoria)

HMS Philomel (1890)

In 1913 the Admiralty agreed to lend *Philomel* to New Zealand as a seagoing training cruiser to form the nucleus of the newly established New Zealand Naval Forces, which was a new division of the Royal Navy.

(Syd Goodman Collection)

PHILOMEL

Pearl Class Twin Screw Third Class Protected Cruiser

Displacement: 2,575 tons **Dimensions**: 265 ft x 41 ft x 15 ft **Speed:** 19 knots **Complement:** 190 **Armament:** 8 x 4.7-inch, 8 x 3-pdr, 4 x 14-inch Torpedo Tubes (1 bow, 1 stern, 2 broadside, all above water)

Laid Down: 9 May 1889 **Launched:** 28 August 1890

1891	10 November, commissioned for the Cape of Good Hope and West Coast of Africa Station, where she was to spend the next 7 years.
1894	18 September, arrived in the Benin River, where hostilities had just begun.
	1 December, recommissioned at Simon's Bay.
1896	Present at the bombardment of Zanzibar.
1898	11 February, arrived Plymouth.
	1 March, given a civic reception at the Town Hall by the citizens of Stovehouse.
	1 December, commissioned again for the Cape.
1899	3 September, ordered to Durban, trouble having broken out with the Boers. Two of her 4.7-inch guns were landed and sent to Ladysmith, and men landed to join the Naval Brigade.
1900	February, more guns landed from the ship.
1901	March, docked at Capetown.
1902	19 February, arrived Plymouth Sound.
	8 March, Naval Brigade medals were presented to crew by H.M. King Edward VII in RN Barracks, Devonport.
	22 March, paid off; ship sailed to Hambroline Dockyard for refit.
1904	7 December, on list of non-effective ships.
1905	6 February, towed to the Firth of Forth.
1906-08	Prepared for further service; sailed for the Mediterranean.
1909-13	East Indies Station, recommissioning at Aden in 1911.
1914	Commissioned as the first representative of the New Zealand Division of the RN. Employed on escort duties between New Zealand and Australia. Later detached to the Indian Ocean to search for German cruiser *Emden*.
1917	16 March, returned to New Zealand to pay off.
1921	1 March, commissioned as a Training Ship. Became Base Ship at Devonport Navy Yard, Auckland.
1946	Offered for sale. A proposed ceremonial disposal did not materialise. Sold for £750 to Strongman Shipping Co. Ltd., of New Zealand.
1947	17 January, arrived Coromandel for stripping.
1949	Her hulk was scuttled off Coromandel, east coast of New Zealand.

EDGAR

Edgar Class Twin Screw First Class Protected Cruiser

Displacement: 7,350 tons **Dimensions**: 360 ft x 60 ft 8 in x 24 ft **Speed:** 19½ knots **Complement:** 540 **Armament:** 2 x 9.2-inch, 10 x 6-inch, 12 x 6-pdr, 5 x 3-pdr, 4 x 18-inch Torpedo Tubes (2 submerged and 2 above water, later removed)

Laid Down: 3 June 1889 **Launched:** 24 November 1890

1893-96	In the Mediterranean, then to China.
1895	13 November, ship's launch capsized at Chemulpo, Korea; 48 men lost.
1897-1900	Transport Service conveying relief crews to China.
1900-02	Devonport.
1903-04	Guardship at Holyhead.
1905-06	Refit at Chatham, and fitted as a Boys' Training Ship.
1907	Again in the Transport Service.
1908-13	Home Fleet.
1913	Training Squadron at Queenstown.
1914	Tenth Cruiser Squadron, Northern Patrol.
1915-16	July, supporting the army in the Dardanelles, and at the evacuation of the Gallipoli peninsula.
1917	In Aegean Squadron on detached duties off the Bulgarian coast.
1918	Gibraltar.
1919	Paid off, laid up at Queenstown.
1921	9 May, sold to T.W. Ward Ltd. Arrived Ward's yard at Morecambe on 3 April, 1923 to be broken up.

Of 7,350 tons and 360 feet long, *Edgar*, became the then largest ship built at Devonport. With her construction, the limiting capacity of the existing building slips had been reached, for the clearance in launching this ship from No.5 slip was but a few inches on each side. Usually, when ships were launched, all the men in the Yard could witness it. However, on many occasions, when permission was granted to leave their work to attend a launch, the men would leave the Yard. So, to witness the launch of *Edgar* only workmen employed on the slip, or in the vicinity were allowed to attend. They were ordered to work overtime during three dinner hours to make up for the 'great privilege' of witnessing the launching of the vessel they had built.

In March 1890 provision was made to light the ships, then under construction, by gas. It was felt that this would be of great benefit whenever overtime was required, particularly during the winter months. The work was carried out by Mr. R.E. Couch of Fore Street, Devonport, at a cost of £500. In November 1892 new gas mains were laid on each side of No.2 slip to provide extra flares for night work. In the next couple of years, experiments were carried out to light the ships in South Yard by electricity. When *Edgar* was fitting out in Keyham Yard, a portable dynamo was placed on board with a boiler alongside. It could light about 350 lamps distributed throughout the ship. It was estimated that to light *Edgar* cost £2 a day, including the wages of the men supervising the plant. This was considered expensive, in spite of the fact that the candles formerly used cost nearly as much.

HMS Edgar (1890)

The Edgar class proved very satisfactory in service with their machinery proving to be exceptionally reliable. For this reason they saw an unusual amount of sea service for ships of their size.

(Syd Goodman Collection)

HMS Aeolus (1891)

Twenty-one of the Apollo class of second-class cruisers were built for the Royal Navy under the 1889 Naval Defence Act, with *HMS Aeolus* being the only one to be built at Devonport. Seven of the class were subsequently converted to minelaying cruisers around 1907.

(T. Ferrers-Walker Collection)

AEOLUS

Apollo Class Twin Screw Second Class Protected Cruiser

Displacement: 3,600 tons **Dimensions**: 300 ft x 43 ft 8 in x 18 ft **Speed:** 18 knots **Complement:** 273 **Armament:** 2 x 6-inch, 6 x 4.7-inch, 8 x Pd, 1 x 3-pdr, 4 x Torpedo Tubes (2 broadside, 1 bow, 1 stern)

Laid Down: 10 March 1890 **Launched:** 13 November 1891

1894	In Mediterranean, then to China in following year.
1897	26 June, at Spithead Review, afterwards paid off at Devonport.
1902	Flagship and Port Guardship at Queenstown.
1903	19 June, commissioned as seagoing Drill Ship for RNR.
1905	September, to Reserve at Devonport.
1906	1 June, grounded on the mud at Milford Haven.
1909	March, arrived Haulbowline for refit.
1910	March, became Tender to *Europa* in Fourth Division of Home Fleet.
	September, conveyed to St. Helena, a new crew for the cruiser *Pandora*.
1911	Replaced *Scylla* in the West Indies.
1912	Training Squadron.
1913	3 October, paid off into Reserve at Chatham.
1914	26 May, sold to T.W. Ward Ltd., of Preston.

Before the ship was laid down on 10 March 1890, No.2 slip was lengthened. Even so, when she launched in November 1891, her bows extended beyond the shed covering the slip. At 21 in number, the Apollo class was numerically the largest class of cruisers ever built for the Royal Navy. They were derived from the earlier Medea class but were more generously proportioned, though quite modestly armed for their size. *HMS Aeolus* was one of ten of the class whose hull was sheathed and coppered for tropical service.

ASTRAEA

Astraea Class Twin Screw Second Class Protected Cruiser

Displacement: 4,360 tons **Dimensions**: 320 ft x 49 ft 6 in x 19 ft **Speed:** 19½ knots **Complement:** 318 **Armament:** 2 x 6-inch, 8 x 4.7-inch, 8 x 6-pdr, 1 x 3-pdr, 4 x 18-inch Torpedo Tubes (2 broadside, 1 bow, 1 stern)

Laid Down: 14 August 1890 **Launched:** 17 March 1893

1895-98	Mediterranean; paid off at Devonport 5 December, 1898.
1898-99	Refit at Chatham. Afterwards commissioned for the Mediterranean.
1900	Transferred to China Station, arriving Hong Kong 21 October.
1901	Guardship at Shanghai.
1902	Paid off at Chatham on 12 June.
1903	Refit at Glasgow.
1904	25 February, commissioned at Chatham, again for the Mediterranean.
	July, ordered to China.
1906	20 September, recommissioned at Hong Kong.
1908	8 February, recommissioned at Colombo.
1912	30 June, paid off at Sheerness, and recommissioned with a reduced crew as Tender to *Albion* at the Nore.
1913	22 April, commissioned for the Cape of Good Hope Station.
1914-18	Most of World War 1 was spent on the Cape Station.
1914	8 August, with *Pegasus*, destroyed wireless station, sank a floating dock and *Mowed* at Dar-es-Salaam.
1919	1 July, paid off.
1920	July, sold to Mr. S. Castle.
1922	September, left Sheerness to be broken up in Germany.

The eight ships of the Astraea class were ordered under the provisions of the 1889 Naval Defence Act as an improved design of the preceding Apollo class cruisers. They were to displace 1,000 tons more than the previous class, and were to have improved sea-keeping abilities, and heavier and better placed armament. The low midship freeboard which had so blighted the performance of earlier small cruisers was replaced by a single full length weather deck. All were built at Royal Dockyards; *Astraea*, *Bonaventure* and *Hermione* at Devonport; *Cambrian* and *Flora* at Pembroke; *Charybdis* at Sheerness and *Forte* at Chatham.

HMS Astraea (1893)

Compared to the preceding Apollo class, the Astraea class featured a full length deck that gave a higher freeboard amidships, and placed the main armament higher on the superstructure. Though this made them drier ships, the design was criticised for being a larger and more expensive development of the Apollos, but without offering any substantial increase in armament, speed or endurance.

(Syd Goodman Collection)

HMS Bonaventure (1892)

Early service took her to the China Station and the Pacific. Although quickly obsolete, the Astraea class ships were quite economical and they found further service as non-frontline warships. On returning home *Bonaventure* was fitted out as a sea-going base ship for submarines.

(*Syd Goodman Collection*)

BONAVENTURE

Astraea Class Twin Screw Second Class Protected Cruiser

Displacement: 4,360 tons **Dimensions**: 320 ft x 49 ft 6 in x 19 ft **Speed:** 19½ knots **Complement:** 318 **Armament:** 2 x 6-inch, 8 x 4.7-inch, 8 x Pd, 1 x 3-pdr, 4 x 18-inch Torpedo Tubes (2 broadside, 1 bow, 1 stern)

Laid Down: 9 December 1890 **Launched:** 2 December 1892

1894	5 July, commissioned for the East Indies Station.
1897	May, returned to Plymouth; then to Naval Review at Spithead.
1898	3 March, commissioned for China Station.
1899	5 July, grounded on east coast of Korea; was docked for repair at Hong Kong.
1901	26 July, arrived Plymouth.
1903-06	On Pacific Station and then in China.
1906-07	Converted at Queenstown to a parent ship for submarines.
1909	July, whilst escorting her flotilla of submarines from the Humber to Southend, they were run into by SS *Eddystone*; *C11* was sunk, *C16* and *C17* collided with one another; the latter was towed to Sheerness by *Bonaventure*.
1910	Carried out wireless communication trials with submarine *D1*.
1911	Escorted HM Submarines *C36, C37* and *C38* (bound for China) as far as Malta.
1912	October, became Submarine Depot Ship at Harwich.
1914	Humber.
1914-16	Submarine Depot Ship to Sixth Submarine Squadron on Tyne.
1916-18	Submarine Depot Ship to Second Submarine Squadron on Tyne.
1919	On the Sales List.
1920	12 April, was sold to the Forth Shopbreaking Company, and broken up at Bo'ness in the following October.

ANTELOPE

Alarm Class Twin Screw First Class Torpedo Gunboat

Displacement: 810 tons **Dimensions**: 230 ft x 27 ft x 8 ft 9 in **Speed:** 18.6 knots **Complement:** 91 **Armament:** 2 x 4,7-inch, 4 x 3-pdr, 3 x 18-inch Torpedo Tubes (1 bow and 2 revolving broadside tubes)

Laid Down: 21 October 1889 **Launched:** 12 July 1893

Construction was delayed because of the shortage of shipwrights and non-availability of a contractor to build her machinery. However, much of her machinery was on board, and her funnels shipped, when she was launched.

1899	4 May, first commissioned; used for training of RNR.
1904	December, relieved in above role by *Hussar*.
1905	26 January, towed from Devonport to lie amongst other ineffective ships at Motherbank, Spithead.
1909	October, to Pembroke for refit.
1910	25 June, commissioned for duty with submarines at Portsmouth.
1912	Paid off at Portsmouth; returned to Devonport for Disposal List in 1916.
1919	27 May, sold to T.R. Sales for £3,500.

Under the Naval Defence Act of 1889, provision was made for the construction of eighteen Torpedo Gunboats. One of the first, *Antelope,* was on the slipway a considerable time due to the shortage shipwrights and because contractors could not be found willing to build the machinery. This was eventually undertaken by Messrs. Yarrow, of Poplar in 1892 and the ship was eventually launched on 12 July 1893. The shortage of shipwrights had arisen because that year, 1889, had seen the laying down of the Third Class Protected Cruisers *Phoebe* (in April) and *Philomel* (in May). The situation was further complicated with the laying down, in June, of the First Class Protected Cruiser, *Edgar*.

The ship was launched by Miss Crocker, the daughter of the shipyard manager. In 2015, her grandson displayed a commemorative wooden box, holding the mallet and chisel she used to sever the rope tethering the ship, on the BBC programme *Antiques Roadshow*.

HERMIONE

Astraea Class Twin Screw Second Class Protected Cruiser

Displacement: 4,360 tons **Dimensions**: 320 ft x 49 ft 6 in x 19 ft
Speed: 19½ knots **Complement:** 318
Armament: 2 x 6-inch, 8 x 4.7-inch, 8 x 6-pdr, 1 x 3-pdr, 4 x 18-inch
Torpedo Tubes (2 broadside, 1 bow, 1 stern)

Laid Down: 17 December 1891 **Launched:** 7 November 1893

1895	Trials in the Channel and Stokes Bay.
1896	In Particular Service Squadron.
1897-98	In the Channel Squadron.
1898-1901	On the China Station.
1902	7 May, recommissioned at Malta to spend the next 2 years in the Mediterranean.
1904	5 August, arrived Devonport; paid off into Reserve; later in Reserve at Portsmouth.
1907	Became Senior Officer's ship on East Coast of Africa.
1909	14 February, grounded on the coast of Zanzibar, for which her Commanding Officer and Navigating Officer were court martialled and reprimanded. Repairs required docking at Capetown. August, ran aground in the Humber.
1910-12	Used in experiments with airships and with aircraft landing and taking off from the sea at Barrow-in-Furness.
1913	17 July, commissioned for the Fourth Cruiser Squadron in the Western Atlantic.
1914	Depot Ship at Southampton for patrol vessels. Two of her 4.7-inch guns were removed, mounted each side of the lighthouse on South Pierhead at Avonmouth, and manned by the Army.
1921	25 October, sold to the Multilocular Shipbreaking Company, Stranraer. 18 December, purchased by the Marine Society and, with all machinery removed, was adapted as Boys' Training Ship.
1922-39	Replaced *Warspite*, in the Thames, which had been burned previously; she adopted the name *Warspite*.
1940	September, sold to T.W. Ward Ltd., Gravesend.

HMS Hermione (1893)

The decommissioned *Hermione* was sold to the Marine Society in 1922 and became the training ship *Warspite*, surviving to September 1940.

(Syd Goodman Collection)

HMS Harrier (1894)

At over 262 feet long these torpedo gunboats were not small ships by the standard of the time; they were larger than the majority of World War I destroyers.

(Naval Heritage & History Command NHHC60578)

HARRIER

Dryad Class Twin Screw First Class Torpedo Gunboat

Displacement: 1,070 tons **Dimensions**: 250 ft x 30 ft 6 in x 9 ft **Speed:** 19 knots **Complement:** 120 **Armament:** 2 x 4.7-inch, 4 x 6-pdr, 5 x 18-inch Torpedo Tubes (1 bow and 2 double revolving broadside tubes)

Laid Down: 2 January 1893 **Launched:** 20 February 1894

Her laying down was delayed because of the shortage of shipwrights.

Her launching was brought forward to allow *Talbot* to be laid down in the current financial year.

1895	On completion of trials was placed in Reserve.
1897	14 January, first commissioned for service in the Mediterranean.
1900	1 March, arrived Devonport; paid off into Reserve.
1901-04	In the Mediterranean; recommissioned at Malta 5 April, 1904.
1905	Fishery Protection duties off the coast of Scotland.
	27 July, touched ground when leaving Aberdeen; required docking there.
1906-13	Appropriated for service with the Navigation School at Portsmouth.
1914	With *Niger* and 6 tugs formed the Downs Boarding Flotilla.
1919	Laid up at Haulbowline; placed on the Disposal List.
1920	23 February, sold to Venezuelan agents, but was arrested and passed into the custody of the Admiralty Marshal.
1921	1 September, auctioned; sold for £1,350 to a Welsh firm who proposed to convert her to commercial use.

The five Dryad class torpedo gunboats, three of which were built at Devonport, were the last class of torpedo gunboat built for the Royal Navy. This type of vessel was rapidly replaced by the faster torpedo boat destroyer, and all of the class were converted to minesweepers during World War I, with the exception of *Hazard*, which became a submarine depot ship.

HALCYON

Dryad Class Twin Screw First Class Torpedo Gunboat

Displacement: 1,070 tons **Dimensions**: 250 ft x 30 ft 6 in x 9 ft **Speed:** 19 knots **Complement:** 120 **Armament:** 2 x 4.7-inch, 4 x 6-pdr, 5 x 18-inch Torpedo Tubes (1 bow and 2 double revolving broadside tubes)

Laid Down: 2 January 1893 **Launched:** 6 April 1894

Her laying down was delayed because of the shortage of shipwrights.

1894	Used in trials of various types of propeller.
1895-98	In the Channel Squadron replacing *Sharpshooter*.
1898-1901	In the Mediterranean.
1901-02	In Reserve at Devonport.
1903-04	Major refit at Messrs. Laird Bros, at Birkenhead. She was re-engined and re-boilered.
1904	Became mother ship to torpedo boats and destroyers at Portsmouth.
1905	Service with North Sea Fisheries, the Commanding Officer of *Halcyon* being the Senior Naval Officer (SNO). December, in collision with *Orotava*; docked at Sheerness for repairs.
1908-14	Under orders of the Admiral Commanding the Coastguard.
1914	August, established the naval base at Lowestoft. November, damaged in action with the German Fleet making their first raid of the war on the English coast.
1915	Patrols in the North Sea, during which she carried a Schneider seaplane.
1917	29 July, rammed and sank the German *UB-27* north of Lowestoft.
1919	6 November, sold for £6,500 to J.H. Lee of Dover.

HMS Halcyon (1894)

HMS Halcyon was engined by Hawthorn Leslie and Company with two sets of vertical triple-expansion steam engines, two locomotive-type boilers, and twin screws. She produced 6,000 indicated horsepower, nearly twice the power of the rest of her class.

(Naval Heritage & History Command NHHC75949)

HMS Hussar (1894)

When built *HMS Hussar* carried a different armament from the rest of the class, namely a single 4.7-inch gun, two 12-pdrs and a single 6-pdr. Between 1896 and 1905 she served on the Mediterranean station.

(Naval Heritage & History Command NHHC60595)

HUSSAR

Dryad Class Twin Screw First Class Torpedo Gunboat

Displacement: 1,070 tons **Dimensions**: 250 ft x 30 ft 6 in x 9 ft **Speed:** 19 knots **Complement:** 120 **Armament:** 1 x 4.7-inch, 2 x 12-pdr, 1 x 6-pdr, 5 x 18-inch Torpedo Tubes (1 bow and 2 double revolving broadside tubes)

Laid Down: 3 April 1893 **Launched:** 3 July 1894

1896-99	In the Mediterranean.
1900	19 February, returned to Devonport; then to Haulbowline for refit.
1901-04	Again in the Mediterranean.
1904	15 January, arrived Devonport; recommissioned the next forenoon and sailed the same afternoon back to the Mediterranean.
1905	3 January, commissioned as a Drill Ship for the RNR.
	Later in the year she was employed on Fishery Protection duties.
1906	In Reserve at Chatham.
1907	Her guns were removed and she was used as an Admiral's Yacht in the Mediterranean.
1909	March-April, refitted at Malta when her forecastle gun was replaced to render her suitable for patrol work.
1914	In the Dardanelles, where her Commanding Officer, Cdr. E. Urwin, won the Victoria Cross.
1916	In the Aegean.
1919-20	Again served as a Yacht and Despatch Vessel for the C-in-C, Mediterranean.
1920	December, sold to Eduardo Jaunch.
1921	13 July, re-sold to Luigi Gatt to be broken up in Malta.

TALBOT

Eclipse Class Twin Screw Second Class Protected Cruiser

Displacement: 5,600 tons **Dimensions**: 350 ft x 53 ft 6 in x 20 ft 6 in **Speed:** 19½ knots **Complement:** 437 **Armament:** 5 x 6-inch, 6 x 4.7-inch, 8 x 12-pdr, 7 x 3-pdr (re-armed in 1904-05 with 11 x 6-inch), 3 x 18-inch Torpedo Tubes (2 submerged and one above water in the stern)

Laid Down: 5 March 1894 **Launched:** 25 April 1895

1896	15 September, commissioned for the North America and West Indies Station. There she was fired upon by the Americans during the Spanish-American War.
1899	23 November, paid off at Devonport.
1901	10 April, commissioned for China; her departure was delayed to allow the fitting of 'wireless telegraphy' apparatus.
1904	9 February, the crew were eye-witnesses to the destruction of the Russian cruiser *Varyag* and gunboat *Korietz* by the Japanese. She took on board some of the survivors.
1904	16 July, returned to Devonport; then to Chatham for refit, where she was re-armed with 11 x 6-inch guns in place of the original 6-inch & 4.7-inch weapons.
1907	Joined the Channel Fleet.
1909-10	In the Second Division of the Home Fleet.
1912	Attached 8th BS, Third Fleet. Employed conveying service reliefs overseas. November, Ran aground in Suez Canal whilst trooping.
1913	She was temporarily the parent ship for the Seventh Destroyer Flotilla.
1914	At the outbreak of war, she joined the 12th Cruiser Squadron. The squadron convoyed to Plymouth the first contingent of 33,000 Canadians in 32 liners, arriving Plymouth on 14 October, 1914.
1915	April, part of the support force which landed troops on 'W' beach at Cape Hellas on the Gallipoli peninsula. Also played a vital role in the bombardments in the Dardanelles.
1916-17	Transferred to the East Africa Station.
1919	13 May, paid off; laid up at Haulbowline.
1921	6 December, sold to the Multilocular Shipbreaking Co., Stranraer.

One of nine Eclipse class cruisers they were expanded Astraeas with an additional 1,000 tons displacement intended to improve seakeeping. Like the earlier Astraea class they were initially criticised for not making greater advantage of their increased size by mounting a heavier armament. Between 1902-04 all, except *Eclipse*, were re-armed with a uniform battery of eleven 6-inch guns.

HMS Talbot (1895)

In World War I *HMS Talbot* landed troops on the Gallipoli peninsula and also played a vital role during the bombardments in the Dardanelles, earning the Battle Honour Dardanelles 1915-16.

(*Syd Goodman Collection*)

PHOENIX

Phoenix Class Steel Twin Screw Sloop

Displacement: 1,050 tons **Dimensions**: 185 ft x 32 ft 6 in x 11 ft 3 in **Speed:** 12.7 knots **Complement:** 106 **Armament:** 6 x 4-inch, 4 x 3-pdr

Laid Down: 26 July 1894 **Launched:** 25 April 1895

1897	11 February commissioned for China, never to return.
1904	14 December, paid off.
1906	18 September, during a typhoon which hit Hong Kong, *Phoenix* was struck by the C.P.R. vessel *Monteagle* and both ended up on shore. *Phoenix* became a total wreck.
1907	7 January, her wreck was sold at a public auction.

ALGERINE

Phoenix Class Steel Twin Screw Sloop

Displacement: 1,050 tons **Dimensions**: 185 ft x 32 ft 6 in x 11 ft 3 in **Speed:** 12.7 knots **Complement:** 106 **Armament:** 6 x 4-inch, 4 x 3-pdr

Laid Down: 25 July 1894 **Launched:** 6 June 1895

1897	11 February, commissioned to relieve *Swift* in China.
1900	13 April, recommissioned at Hong Kong. Took part in the Third China War, including the bombardment of the Taku forts.
1905-08	On the Sales List at Hong Kong.
1908	5 March, recommissioned for patrol duties in the Bering Sea.
1913	December, recommissioned at Esquimault, for last time in RN.
1914	Handed over to Canada, and throughout World War 1 acted as Depot Ship for the Esquimault Base.
1919	11 April, sold to the British Columbia Salvage Company.
1924	January, sold for scrap.

The Phoenix class was a two-ship class of steel twin-screw sloops for the Royal Navy, both of which were built at Devonport. At the time of completion screw sloops such as these had been obsolete for many years, but they remained ideal for patrolling Britain's extensive maritime interests overseas, and both *Phoenix* and *Algerine* were deployed to the China Station. Both ships participated in the suppression of the Boxer Rebellion.

HMS Algerine (1895)

The Phoenix class was a two-ship class of sloops, both built at Devonport. They were constructed of steel and powered by both barquentine-rigged sails and a twin-screw steam engine developing 1,400 horsepower. *HMS Algerine* was launched in 1895 and saw action in China during the Boxer Rebellion.

(T. Ferrers-Walker Collection)

HMS Arrogant (1896)

HMS Arrogant sporting an all over grey colour scheme which replaced the black hull, white superstructure and buff funnels and masts of the early Victorian era.

(T. Ferrers-Walker Collection)

ARROGANT

Arrogant Class Twin Screw Second Class Protected Cruiser

Displacement: 5,800 tons **Dimensions**: 320 ft x 57 ft 6 in x 21 ft **Speed:** 19.1 knots **Complement:** 480 **Armament:** 4 x 6-inch, 6 x 4.7-inch, 9 x 12-pdr, 3 x 3-pdr (re-armed in 1906 with 10 x 6-inch), 2 x 18-inch Torpedo Tubes (submerged)

Laid Down: 10 June 1895 **Launched:** 26 May 1896

1897	September, on trials which were conducted by naval ratings as the machinery contractor's men were on strike.
1898	27 January, commissioned for the Channel Squadron.
	18 August, carried out gunnery tests against a dummy 9.2-inch gun erected on Steep Holm island in the Bristol Channel.
1899	16 September, towed Training Ship *Ganges* to Sheerness.
1901	September, after refit at Devonport, sailed to Lagos.
1903	3 November, commissioned for the Mediterranean.
1905	Nine months in Reserve before commissioning into Atlantic Fleet.
1909	14 September, commissioned for Special Service - conveying relief crews to Malta.
1911	1 July, commissioned as Depot Ship for Submarines at Portsmouth.
1914-18	Flagship of Vice-Admiral Sir Roger Keyes, Dover Patrol.
1919	25 March, arrived in tow at Devonport to await disposal.
1923	11 October, sold to Hughes Bolckow Ltd. and broken up at Blyth.

The 1895-96 programme of naval construction included provision for four Second Class Protected Cruisers. The Arrogant class were different to their contemporaries in so much as they were designed to be operated with the main battle fleet, rather than in the more traditional trade protection duties. Originally described as Fleet Rams, the Arrogant class ships were designed to finish off damaged enemy ships by ramming. For this, armour (3-inch reducing to 2-inch underwater) covered the whole bow, narrowing as it ran aft. The 160 tons of armour used produced a reinforced bow regarded as the strongest ram bow yet built. Aft of the ram was a pair of collision bulkheads which extended right up to the upperdeck. The void forward of the bulkheads was further subdivided to provide increased watertight integrity, while the space between the two bulkheads contained cork-filled cofferdams. To enable the ships to get close to their targets their conning position was protected by 9-inch armour to afford some degree of protection from incoming enemy shellfire and they were fitted with a second rudder further forward to give them increased manoeuvrability - they were capable of turning within a diameter of 38 yards, comparing favourably with the 650 yards of the earlier Astraea class.

FURIOUS

Arrogant Class Twin Screw Second Class Protected Cruiser

Displacement: 5,750 tons **Dimensions**: 320 ft x 57 ft 6 in x 21 ft **Speed:** 19.1 knots **Complement:** 480 **Armament:** 4 x 6-inch, 6 x 4.7-inch, 8 x 12-pdr, 3 x 3-pdr, 2 x 18-inch Torpedo Tubes (submerged)

Laid Down: 10 June 1895 **Launched:** 3 December 1896

Designed as a ram and fitted with a double rudder.

1898	1 July, commissioned into the Channel Squadron.
1903	During refit at Chatham, she was re-armed and re-boilered.
1903-05	In the Mediterranean.
1905	6 January, commissioned as a Tender to *HMS Vernon*, the Torpedo School at Portsmouth.
1911	October-November, carried out wireless experiments in the Mediterranean.
1912	Reduced to Harbour Service at Portsmouth.
1913-15	Laid up, Motherbank.
1915	June, renamed *Forte* and again attached to *Vernon* as a hulk.
1923	May, sold to G. Cohen, of Swansea.

The Arrogant class were the first Royal Navy Second Class Cruisers to use water-tube boilers, with 18 Belleville boilers feeding triple-expansion steam engines which drove two shafts, giving a service speed of 18 knots. They were heavily criticised at the time as being too slow and under-armed in comparison to ships in service with Germany, or with those being built for export. The issue of being under-armed was addressed in 1904 when the ship's armament was replaced by a battery of ten 6-inch guns.

While the Devonport pair of *Arrogant* and *Furious* survived the war, the Portsmouth ships, *Gladiator* and *Vindictive* fared less well. During a late snowstorm off the Isle of Wight on 25 April 1908, *Gladiator* was heading into port when she struck the outbound American steamer SS *Saint Paul*. Although visibility was down to 800 yds the strong tides and gale force winds required both ships to maintain high speeds to maintain steerage. *Gladiator* was hit just aft of the engine room and the sudden in rush of water saw her rapidly roll over onto her starboard side with 27 sailors being lost. Although the ship was eventually salvaged some months later she was deemed a total loss and never returned to service. During WWI *Vindictive* was central to both the Zeebrugge and Ostend operations, finally being sunk as a block ship at the latter. She was raised after the war and a section of her bow now serves as a memorial at Ostend.

HMS Furious (1896)

HMS Furious was paid off in 1912. She was renamed *HMS Forte* in 1915, and served as a hulk attached to *HMS Vernon*, the Royal Navy's Torpedo School, at Portsmouth.

(Allan C. Green courtesy of the State Library of Victoria)

HMS Ocean (1898)

Although her launching weight was not the heaviest on record, she was heavier per foot length than any vessel hitherto launched in a Government Yard. To reduce the risk at her launch, the slip was further extended by 20-30 feet into the Hamoaze, by dredging the entrance to the slip and extending the concrete bed. She was launched by HRH Princess Louise.

(*Ken Kelly Collection*)

OCEAN

Canopus Class Battleship

Displacement: 12,950 tons **Dimensions**: 390 ft x 74 ft 6 in x 26 ft **Speed:** 18.3 knots **Complement:** 750 **Armament:** 4 x 12-inch, 12 x 6-inch, 12 x 12-pdr, 6 x 3-pdr (re-armed in 1906 with 10 x 6-inch), 4 x 18-inch Torpedo Tubes (submerged)

Laid Down: 15 February 1897 **Launched:** 5 July 1898

1900	20 February, commissioned for the Mediterranean.
1901	February, left Malta for China in consequence of the Boxer outbreak.
1903	After 6 months refit in Hong Kong, there was an outbreak of plague on board; ship was placed in quarantine during June and July.
1905	2 August, returned to Devonport; paid off on the 16th.
1906	In the Channel Fleet.
1908-10	In the Mediterranean.
1911-12	Home Fleet, part of the Eighth Battle Squadron of Third Fleet.
1913	At Pembroke Dock.
1914	Sent to the East Indies.
	October-November, took part in Persian Gulf operations.
1915	February-March, in the Dardanelles.
	18 March, in the Dardanelles. *Ocean*, along with 2 other battleships - *HMS Irresistible* and the French *Bouvet* - were sunk by drifting mines. The ship's company of *Ocean* were taken off by destroyers. The ship drifted into Morto Bay and she sank about 2230.

To enable the *Ocean* to be built one of the slipways had to be lengthened. In June 1896 the Admiralty invited tenders to extend No.3 slip which had just had its roof taken off. The wood covering provided protection from the rain so some of the men did not relish the prospect of being subjected to all winds and weathers. On the other hand shipbuilding on open slipways commended itself to other men because the conditions were far more healthy than being under cover. Work on the extension commenced in August 1896.

Much preliminary work on *Ocean* was done before the ship's keel was laid on 15 February 1897. Instructions were given that she be completed within 20 months. An incentive in hastening her construction was what became known as 'The Canopus Stakes' a shipbuilding race between the Royal Dockyards building Canopus class battleships - *Canopus* at Portsmouth; *Goliath* at Chatham and *Ocean* at Devonport. Devonport started five weeks after the other two Yards and suffered a serious set-back when some of the ship's frames collapsed. It appears that the framework had been left insecure when two gangs of men were removed to assist in docking the battleship *Colossus*. The ribs of the ship fell like a pack of cards; about 90 feet of the fore part of the ship - from the stem to the turret - collapsed, over 100 tons of material being dislodged. At the official inquiry, a labourer confessed that he removed a bolt which had been keeping some frames in position until the plating and riveting had been completed. The man was ignorant of the consequences of his action, his object in removing the bolt being to facilitate the passage of some iron plates he was conveying to another part of the ship. An examination of the loosened bolt showed it to be intact - that it had been unscrewed - and not wrenched off.

Other vexatious delays occurred - shortage of drillers and riveters; a strike in the engineering trades; non-delivery of the principal castings such as the stem, stern post, rudder, shaft brackets etc. Consequently *Ocean* was on the slip for 17 months, twice as long as expected.

PSYCHE

Pelorus Class Twin Screw Third Class Protected Cruiser

Displacement: 2,135 tons **Dimensions**: 300 ft x 36 ft 6 in x 17 ft 6 in **Speed:** 19 knots **Complement:** 224 **Armament:** 8 x 4-inch, 8 x 3-pdr, 2 x 14-inch Torpedo Tubes (broadside, above water)

Laid Down: 16 November 1897 **Launched:** 19 July 1898

1899-1902	First commission on the North America and West Indies Station.
1902	November, proceeded to Hawthorn, Leslie at Newcastle for refit.
1903	23 September, commissioned for the Australian Station, never to return home again. She recommissioned at Trincomalee in 1905, at Singapore in 1907, and at Colombo in 1909 and 1911.
1913	Transferred to the New Zealand Station.
1914	15 July, recommissioned at Wellington.
	August, with *Philomel* and *Pyramus*, she escorted the N.Z. Expeditionary Force which occupied Samoa.
1915	Lent to the Royal Australian Navy; commissioned at Sydney on 1 July, for the training of seamen and stokers.
1918	Paid off.
1922	21 July, sold at Sydney to the Waterside Ship Chandlery and Shipping Co., of Melbourne for breaking up.

In 1898 it was planned to make extensive alterations to No.5 slip, the northernmost one from which *Psyche* had been launched on 19 July, in order to provide facilities for the building of a second battleship. The only slip then available for such a purpose was No.3 on which the keel of *Implacable* had been laid six days earlier. However, a survey of No.5 slip satisfied the authorities that the extension was impracticable as the work would have involved the demolition of the Smithery and other permanent buildings.

An alternative scheme, the building of an entirely new slip, was undertaken at a point which had the advantage that vessels built on it would be launched into the widest part of the Hamoaze. Situated between two old building sheds at the southern end of the Yard (No.1 and No.2 slips) and No.3 slip, on which *Ocean* and *Montagu* were built, were the old mast ponds and timber sheds. These facilities had been well suited for the building of wooden ships, but had then become obsolete. The mast ponds were accordingly filled in and a considerably sized area of land cleared, including the timber houses and plank sheds.

Work on clearing the site commenced in July 1900. The original plan was for a slip 450 feet in length but after the work had started the dimensions were increased to 600 feet long by 90 feet wide. Furthermore, allowance was also made in the foundations for any future extensions up to 155 feet. The gradient of the slip was 1 in 19, with the head of the slip about 30ft above rock level. The new slip was numbered No.3 and the old No.3 was re-numbered No.4 slip.

HMS Psyche (1898)

Unlike the earlier Eclipse class, the Pelorus class reverted to a raised forecastle and poop design, presenting a low freeboard amidships. Consequently these ships, once again, proved to be quite wet in service.

(Syd Goodman Collection)

HMS Implacable (1899)

Although based on the Majestic class, the Formidables presented an improved Canopus design ranking as the most powerful European battleship model of their day.

(Syd Goodman Collection)

IMPLACABLE

Formidable Class Battleship

Displacement: 15,000 tons **Dimensions**: 400 ft x 75 ft x 25 ft **Speed:** 18 knots **Complement:** 700 **Armament:** 4 x 12-inch, 12 x 6-inch, 16 x 12-pdr, 6 x 3-pdr, 4 x 18-inch Torpedo Tubes (submerged)

Laid Down: 13 July 1898 **Launched:** 11 March 1899

1901	10 September, first commissioned by Captain Prince Louis of Battenburg, GCB, GCVO, for service in the Mediterranean.
1904	31 August, returned to Devonport to pay off.
1904-08	Two further commissions in the Mediterranean.
1905	12 July, off Gibraltar, a boiler explosion killed 7.
1906	16 August, another boiler explosion.
1908	29 May, paid off at Devonport.
1909	Refit at Chatham.
1910-11	In the Atlantic Fleet; and later the Channel Fleet.
1912	13 May, reduced to nucleus crew in the Second Fleet at the Nore.
1914	Fifth Battle Squadron in the Second Fleet.
1915	In the Dardanelles, with *Queen*, to replace *Ocean* and *Irresistible* which had been sunk.
1916-17	In the Mediterranean. She was the last of the fully commissioned battleships to operate there in the War.
1918	Northern Patrol. Paid off in the summer of 1919.
1919-20	Tender to *Research*, a surveying vessel at Portland.
1920	24 April, to Portsmouth to prepare for sale.
1921	8 November, sold to Slough Trading Co., of London; broken up in Germany in April, 1922.

Work on *Implacable* actually commenced on No.2 slip, her frames being bolted together so that they could easily be taken down and moved to No.3 slip after *Ocean* had been launched. *Implacable* was launched on 11 March 1899 in the presence of the Crown Prince of Siam. The three Formidable class battleships were, in appearance, heavier looking editions of the Canopus class, with funnels wider apart and an extra 12-pdr gun aside in the battery. By 1916, *Implacable* was the sole survivor of the class and had her main deck 6-inch battery plated in, four of the guns being placed a deck higher in the former 12-pdr battery, where they were fired through large ports with light shield protection. The 12-pdrs were reduced to eight and moved to the shelter decks.

BULWARK

London Class First Class Armoured Battleship

Displacement: 15,000 tons **Dimensions**: 400 ft x 75 ft x 26 ft 9 in **Speed:** 18 knots **Complement:** 750 **Armament:** 4 x 12-inch, 12 x 6-inch, 16 x 12-pdr, 6 x 3-pdr, 4 x 18-inch Torpedo Tubes (submerged)

Laid Down: 20 March 1899 **Launched:** 18 October 1899

1902-04	Flagship of C-in-C Mediterranean (Admiral Sir Compton E. Domvile).
1905-07	Flagship of C-in-C Mediterranean (Admiral Lord Charles Beresford).
1907	12 February, commissioned as Flagship of Rear Admiral in command of Home Fleet at the Nore.
	26 October, grounded about 10 miles S.E. of Leman light in North Sea; required docking for repairs.
1908	30 May, Captain R.F. Scott, of Antarctic fame, joined her - the most junior Captain in command of a battleship.
1910-11	Flagship of Vice Admiral commanding the Third and Fourth Divisions of the Home Fleet.
1911-12	Refit at Chatham.
1912	May, during post-refit trials she twice grounded on Barrow Deep off the Nore.
1914	In Fifth Battle Squadron.
	26 November, whilst embarking ammunition at Sheerness she was destroyed by an internal explosion which cost the lives of almost the entire ship's company - only 12 were saved.

The London class was regarded as a transitional battleship between the Formidables and Duncans, incorporating some of the modifications which had been accepted for the later Duncans.

MONTAGU

Duncan Class Battleship

Displacement: 14,000 tons **Dimensions**: 405 ft x 75 ft 6 in x 25 ft 9 in **Speed:** 18 knots **Complement:** 750 **Armament:** 4 x 12-inch, 12 x 6-inch, 12 x 12-pdr, 6 x 3-pdr, 4 x 18-inch Torpedo Tubes (submerged)

Laid Down: 23 November 1899 **Launched:** 5 March 1901

1903	28 July, first commissioned for the Mediterranean.
1905	February, joined the Channel Fleet.
1906	Employed in the Bristol Channel testing appliances designed to prevent wireless messages being tapped.
	30 May, in dense fog she struck upon the Shutters on the southwest end of Lundy Island. No lives were lost.
	August, salvage operations were abandoned. Her 12-inch guns were removed and landed at Pembroke Dock and shipped to Woolwich; many other stores were salvaged. Her torpedo tubes were destroyed with explosive charges. At a Court Martial, her CO and Navigating Officer were both found guilty, severely reprimanded and dismissed their ship.
1907	February, the wreck was sold to Messrs. Vasey of London, shipbreakers, for £4,250.

HMS Montagu (1901)

The Duncan class battleship was designed in response to a threat posed by a group of alleged fast Russian battleships of the Peresviet class of 1898. In fact the intelligence was faulty, the Russian ships being second class vessels armed with 10-inch and 6-inch guns with moderate protection and a speed of only 16 knots.

(T. Ferrers-Walker Collection)

HMS Queen (1902)

HMS Queen and her sister ship *Prince of Wales* were the last two London-class ships built, but were laid down after the Duncan class battleships that succeeded. This later construction, coupled with their lower displacement, slightly differing armament and a few other minor design differences, lead some authors to view them as constituting a Queen class separate from the Formidable and London classes.

(Ken Kelly Collection)

QUEEN

London Class First Class Armoured Battleship

Displacement: 15,000 tons **Dimensions**: 400 ft x 75 ft x 26 ft **Speed:** 18 knots **Complement:** 750 **Armament:** 4 x 12-inch, 12 x 6-inch, 16 x 12-pdr, 6 x 3-pdr, 4 x 18-inch Torpedo Tubes (submerged)

Laid Down: 12 March 1901 **Launched:** 8 March 1902

Her launching, when she was named by H.M. Queen Alexandra, was immediately followed by the laying of the keel plate of *King Edward VII* by His Majesty.

1904-07	7 April, first commissioned for the Mediterranean.
1906	8 May, commissioned at Portsmouth for another year in the Mediterranean.
1907	5 March, commissioned at Devonport to become Flagship of C-in-C, Mediterranean.
1908	15 December, Commissioned for the Atlantic Fleet.
1910	15 December - recommissioned again for the Atlantic Fleet.
1912	15 May, commissioned as Flagship of Second and Third Fleets.
1914	Operations in the Channel and off the Belgian coast.
1915	March, with *Implacable*, was ordered to the Dardanelles to replace *Ocean* and *Irresistible* which had been sunk.
	May, ordered to the Adriatic to support the Italian forces.
1916-17	Base Ship at Taranto for the anti-submarine Net Barrage Flotilla (comprising 30 motor launches and 120 net drifters).
1919	Returned to England, paying off at Chatham on 21 November.
1920	Prepared for sale at Chatham; then removed to Sheerness.
	4 November, sold to T.W. Ward Ltd., of Preston, who removed her to Birkenhead for stripping and Preston for breaking up.

Their Majesties King Edward VII and Queen Alexandra visited Devonport on 8 March 1902 for a double ceremony. The Queen named the battleship *Queen* at the second attempt, her first attempt at breaking the bottle of Colonial wine having failed. As the ship cleared the slipway, the King pressed a button to set in motion the machinery which, by means of a wire hawser, hauled a steel plate into position on the specially prepared fifteen sets of blocks which had been painted red, white and blue. The plate was decorated with four miniature Union Jacks, one at each corner. In a loud clear voice, His Majesty said, "I declare the first keel-plate of the *King Edward VII* well and truly laid."

ENCOUNTER

Challenger class twin screw second class protected cruiser

Displacement: 5,800 tons **Dimensions**: 355 ft x 56 ft x 20 ft 3 in **Speed:** 21 knots **Complement:** 475 **Armament:** 11 x 6-inch,
8 x 3-inch, 6 x 3-pdr, 2 x 18-inch Torpedo Tubes

Laid Down: 28 January 1901 **Launched:** 18 June 1902

1905-12	Eastern Fleet in Australian waters, recommissioning at Colombo 1 January, 1908 and 15 April, 1910.
1912	1 July, loaned to Australia as a training ship until completion of new cruiser *Brisbane* at Sydney, N.S.W.
1915-16	On patrol between Japan and the Philippines; then based at Singapore to patrol Malayan archipelago. 25 April 1915, captured German sailing vessel *Elfriede*.
1917	Escort duties between New Zealand and Colombo.
1918	Protecting Australian coast between Fremantle and Sydney.
1919	5 December, transferred to Australia for use as a Receiving Ship at Sydney.
1920	February, machinery space flooded by accident.
1923	May, renamed *Penguin*.
1923-29	Submarine Depot Ship until relieved by *Platypus*.
1932	8 September, hulk of *Encounter* scuttled off Bondi, NSW.

The Challenger class was a repeat of the earlier Highflyer class, slightly enlarged to accommodate still more powerful machinery. After *Encounter* had been launched from No.5 slip in 1902, the slip fell into disuse. In 1910 work was taken in hand to convert it and make it suitable for boat repair. A new floor was fitted and massive hauling-up rings were fixed into concrete beds. It provided accommodation for a double line of large boats, which were hauled up the slipway with the aid of 20 hp electrically driven winches.

Two years later though, it was again used for shipbuilding. An oil-carrier for the Royal Fleet Auxiliary, to be named *Carol*, was laid down on 14 November 1912 and after her launch in July 1913 another oiler, *Ferol*, was laid down.

HMS Encounter (1902)

The Challenger class, such as *HMS Encounter*, replaced the Katoombas on the Australian station and represented the ultimate stage in a line of development that began with the Apollos.

(Allan C Green courtesy of the State Library of Australia)

HMS King Edward VII (1903)

The ships of this class were the first British battleships with balanced rudders since the 1870s and were very manoeuvrable. However, they were difficult to keep on a straight course, and this characteristic led to them being nicknamed 'The Wobbly Eight' during their service in the Grand Fleet.

(George Grantham Bain Collection - Library of Congress)

KING EDWARD VII

King Edward VII Class Battleship

Displacement: 16,350 tons **Dimensions**: 425 ft x 78 ft x 25 ft 6 in **Speed:** 18½ knots **Complement:** 777 **Armament:** 4 x 12-inch, 4 x 9.2-inch, 10 x 6-inch, 12 x 12-pdr, 14 x 3-pdr, 5 x 18-inch Torpedo Tubes (4 submerged on the beam and 1 submerged at the stern)

Laid Down: 8 March 1902 **Launched:** 23 July 1903

When launched, H.M. King Edward VII directed that she should always be used as a Flagship. It was ironic that she should be sunk when no Admiral was on board.

1905-07	Flagship of the Atlantic Fleet.
1905	1 March, entered King Edward VII dock at Gibraltar, the first battleship to enter one of the new graving docks there.
1907-09	Flagship of the Channel Fleet.
1909-11	Flagship of the Second Division of the Home Fleet.
1911-12	Flagship of the Third and Fourth Divisions of the Home Fleet.
1912-14	Flagship of the Third Battle Squadron.
1914	August, at Devonport, where two of her 12-inch guns were exchanged.
1916	6 January, she struck a mine whilst under way, in very heavy weather, from Scapa Flow to Belfast for refit. Attempts to take her in tow failed. All the ship's company were transferred to destroyers before the ship turned over and sank.

A report from the Committee of Public Accounts, published in June 1907 revealed that twelve months after the rudder casting for *King Edward VII* was received and built into the ship, the Admiralty were informed by a dismissed employee of the Ayrshire Foundry Company, that on a Sunday, the Management had collected some workmen together and by means of electric welding had concealed a large fault in the casting. The Admiralty decided that the casting should be replaced. The firm denied that there was anything wrong but offered to replace the casting with a new one. This offer was accepted, but the second casting was full of flaws and defects, and a third one proved no better. The Admiralty then decided that the casting should be made in the Dockyard and the cost charged to the contractors. The rumours of this particular transaction and the subsequent loss of other Admiralty orders brought such financial loss to the Ayrshire Foundry Company that it soon became bankrupt.

The King Edward VII class was a direct descendant of the Majestic class, and the first to mount an intermediate battery of four 9.2-inch guns in addition to the standard outfit of 12-inch and 6-inch guns. The 9.2-inch gun was quick-firing and mounted in four single turrets breast the foremast and mainmast.

HIBERNIA

King Edward VII Class Battleship

Displacement: 16,350 tons **Dimensions**: 425 ft x 78 ft x 26 ft **Speed:** 18½ knots **Complement:** 777 **Armament:** 4 x 12-inch, 4 x 9.2-inch, 10 x 6-inch, 14 x 12-pdr, 14 x 3-pdr, 5 x 18-inch Torpedo Tubes (4 submerged on the beam and 1 submerged at the stern)

Laid Down: 6 January 1904 **Launched:** 17 June 1905

The ship was christened with a bottle of whisky. She was the first ship to be received into the new Dockyard extension, the basin being specially flooded for the occasion.

1907-11	Spent 2 commissions as Flagship of Admiral Second in Command, Channel Fleet.
1911	Flagship of Rear Admiral, Home Fleet.
1912	January, in Nore Sub-Division of the Home Fleet.
	April, at Chatham, she was fitted with a wooden runway over her forecastle for use as an aircraft platform.
	2 May, Lt. A.M. Longmore flew from *Hibernia* and landed at Lodmoor.
	9 May, Cdr. C.R. Samson flew off *Hibernia* - the first flight from a moving British warship.
1913-14	The aircraft platform was removed, and she became Flagship of the Third Battle Squadron.
1914	October, captured SS *Oscar II* which had on board the Austrian Ambassador to Japan and his staff, on their way from Tokyo to Rome. He protested and the ship was released.
1915	In the Dardanelles.
1916	Sustained an 8-inch shell hole from Turkish batteries.
1919-21	Accommodation ship at Chatham.
1921	8 November, sold to Stanlee Shipbreaking Company; later re-sold to the Slough Trading Company of London.
1922	November, left Sheerness in tow, to be broken up in Germany.

Hibernia was to have been the first ship built on the new No.3 slip, but when she was due to be laid down, no lifting derricks had been fitted alongside. She was therefore laid down on the old No.3 slip, re-numbered No.4.

In 1912, *Hibernia* was the chosen vessel to conduct a series of historic trials in naval aviation. In January 1912, aviation experiments began at Sheerness aboard the battleship *Africa*, during which the first British launch of an aeroplane from a ship took place. Following these trials from a stationary ship, the next step was to launch an aircraft from a moving ship. Therefore, *Africa* transferred her flying-off equipment, including a runway constructed over her foredeck above her forward 12-inch (305-mm) turret and stretching from her bridge to her bows, to *Hibernia* in May 1912 for further trials. Among these was the first launch of an aeroplane from a warship underway; Commander Samson, flying a Short Improved Biplane became the first man to take off from a ship which was underway by launching from the battleship while it steamed at 10½ knots in Weymouth Bay.

HMS Hibernia (1905)

HMS Hibernia commissioned on 2 January 1907 at Devonport Dockyard for service as flagship of the Rear-Admiral, Atlantic Fleet before transferring to the Channel Fleet for service as Flagship, Rear-Admiral, on 27 February 1907.

(T. Ferrers-Walker Collection)

HMS Minotaur (1906)

HMS Minotaur, as built, with four short funnels, These were raised in 1909 in an effort to eliminate smoke interference on the bridge.

(Syd Goodman Collection)

MINOTAUR

Minotaur Class Armoured Cruiser

Displacement: 14,600 tons **Dimensions**: 490 ft x 75 ft x 28 ft **Speed:** 23 knots **Complement:** 755 **Armament:** 4 x 9.2-inch, 10 x 7.5-inch, 16 x 12-pdr, 5 x 18-inch Torpedo Tubes (submerged)

Laid Down: 2 January 1905 **Launched:** 6 June 1906

At the time, this class were the most heavily armed cruisers in the RN. *Minotaur* was the longest vessel then built in Dockyard.

1907	November, during trials period, when at anchor in Plymouth Sound, an explosion occurred in No.3 coal bunker; 5 men injured.
1908	1 April, commissioned for service in Fifth Cruiser Squadron.
	June, a silver cup was presented to the ship by H.I.M. the Emperor of Russia who hoisted his flag in *Minotaur* after being made an Admiral of the Fleet, RN.
1909	Refitted at Chatham when her funnels were increased in height by 15 ft.
1910	31 January, sailed for the China Station.
1914	6 August, she captured and sank the German merchantman *Elsbeth* with 1,800 tons of coal on board.
	Patrolled Yap Island, Germany's central Pacific base; bombarded the W/T station.
	When the China Squadron was dispersed, *Minotaur* was ordered to the Cape Station.
1915	Returned home to become Flagship of the Second Cruiser Squadron in the Grand Fleet.
1916	Present at Jutland; and later in North Sea operations.
1919	5 February, paid off to Sales List.
1920	12 April, sold to Messrs. T.W. Ward Ltd. for £41,600. July, arrived Milford Haven for breaking up.

On 2 January 1905, the keel of *Minotaur* was laid down to become the first ship built on the new No.3 slip. She was to be followed by *Temeraire* and *Collingwood*. She had been ordered as part of the 1904-05 naval construction programme as the last of three Minotaur Class Armoured Cruisers. She was christened on 6 June 1907 by the Countess of Crewe. They were the last armoured cruisers built for the Royal Navy. They were significantly larger and more heavily armed than their predecessors, but their design was somewhat flawed as their armour protection was reduced in order to compensate for the additional weight of the armament. In service they suffered smoke interference on the bridge and so, in 1909, their funnels were raised by 15 feet.

TEMERAIRE

Bellerophon Class Battleship

Displacement: 18,800 tons **Dimensions**: 490 ft x 82 ft 6 in x 27 ft 3 in **Speed:** 20¾ knots **Complement:** 733 **Armament:** 10 x 12-inch, 16 x 4-inch, 4 x 3-pdr, 3 x 18-inch Torpedo Tubes (2 broadside and 1 submerged at the stern; removed during the 1914-18 war)

Laid Down: 1 January 1907 **Launched:** 24 August 1907

Her completion was delayed because 40 employees of the Engineering Contractors came out on strike from July to September, 1908.

1909	15 May, commissioned for the First Battle Squadron of the Home Fleet.
1912	5 June, arrived Devonport to exchange her 12-inch guns.
1913-14	In Home Fleet until the outbreak of war when she joined the Fourth Battle Squadron.
1915	March, when the Grand Fleet off Scapa Flow were attacked by the German submarine *U-29*, *Temeraire* and *Dreadnought* attempted to ram her. *Dreadnought* succeeded in destroying *U-29*.
1916	31 May, at Jutland but suffered neither damage nor casualties.
1918	In the Mediterranean.
1919	23 April, paid off into Reserve at Devonport.
	September, commissioned as a Cadets' seagoing Training Ship.
1921	23 April, paid off at Rosyth.
	7 December, sold to the Stanlee Shipbreaking Company, of Dover.
1922	February, arrived Dover for breaking up.

According to the two year limit for building armoured ships, *Temeraire* should have been available to commission on 1 January 1909, but in July the previous year forty employees of the contractors working on the engines, Messrs. Hawthorn, Leslie and Co., Newcastle-on-Tyne, came out on strike and did not resume work until the end of September. This was one of the results of the engineers' strike in the north east of England, the Amalgamated Society of engineers calling out their members engaged in work on *Temeraire*. This action delayed *Temeraire's* trials and meant she did not commission until 15 May 1909 to replace *Implacable* in the First Battle Squadron.

HMS Temeraire (1907)

HMS Temeraire, the first post-Dreadnought battleship to be laid down at Devonport cost, including guns, £1,751,144. Machinery and boilers were as in *Dreadnought*, but coal bunkerage was reduced by 252 tons, to 2,648 tons and oil by 278 tons to 842. This reduced the radius of operations by 760 miles.

(Syd Goodman Collection)

HMS Collingwood (1908)

HMS Collingwood was named after Vice-Admiral Cuthbert Collingwood, notable as a partner with Lord Nelson in several of the British victories of the Napoleonic Wars, and frequently as Nelson's successor in commands.

(*Syd Goodman Collection*)

COLLINGWOOD

St. Vincent Class Battleship

Displacement: 19,250 tons **Dimensions**: 500 ft x 84 ft x 27 ft **Speed:** 21 knots **Complement:** 758 **Armament:** 10 x 12-inch, 20 x 4-inch, 4 x 3-pdr, 3 x 18-inch Torpedo Tubes (2 abeam, 1 in the stern which was removed during 1914-18 war)

Laid Down: 3 February 1908 **Launched:** 7 November 1908

1910	19 April, first commissioned for service in First Division of Home Fleet.
1911	February, was holed entering Ferrol harbour; extensively damaged to outer bottom necessitating docking at Devonport.
1912-14	Flagship of First Battle Squadron until being relieved by *Marlborough*.
1916	31 May, performed nobly at Jutland.
1919-20	Attached to the Gunnery School, Devonport, as a Turret Drill Ship.
1921	Accommodation Ship for the *Impregnable* Training Establishment at Devonport.
	September, transferred to Portland to become Tender to *Colossus*, the Boys' Training Establishment.
1922	31 March, paid off at Portsmouth; placed on Sales List.
	12 December, sold to John Cashmore Ltd., of Newport, where she arrived on 3 March, 1923 for breaking up.

The date originally fixed for the keel laying of *Collingwood* was 2 December 1907, but to allow the firms to whom orders had been entrusted every opportunity for ensuring an uninterrupted supply of material when the Dockyard authorities were ready to build it into the ship, it was delayed until 3 February 1908. The arrangements must have worked well, *Collingwood* being launched just nine months later.

After the launch of *Collingwood*, and before the laying down of the next ship, *Invincible*, the Admiralty decided to implement the original plan that the slip could be lengthened when required. However, although extra foundations had been provided for up to 155 feet, the slip was only extended by 90 feet, all above the level of the Yard making the higher end about 10 feet above the roadway.

INDEFATIGABLE

Indefatigable Class Battle Cruiser

Displacement: 18,750 tons **Dimensions**: 555 ft x 80 ft x 25 ft 9 in **Speed:** 25 knots **Complement:** 800 **Armament:** 8 x 12-inch, 16 x 4-inch, 3 x 18-inch Torpedo Tubes (stern tube later removed)

Laid Down: 23 February 1909 **Launched:** 28 October 1909

To permit her building, the slipway was lengthened 90 feet.

1911-13	In First Cruiser Squadron; later the First Battle Cruiser Squadron.
1913	17 June, recommissioned at Devonport; sailed 6 months later to the Mediterranean.
1914	August, patrolled the Straits of Otranto; then in the Dardanelles.
	3 November, bombarded batteries at Cape Hellas.
1915	January-February, refit at Malta; then returned home to join the Grand Fleet.
1916	31 May, sunk at Jutland when in a duel with the German *Von Der Tann*. Her magazine exploded; only 2 survivors who were rescued by a German destroyer.

The Indefatigable class were the second class built of British battlecruisers which served in the Royal Navy and the Royal Australian Navy during World War I, following the Invincible class. The Indefatigable class was essentially an enlarged Invincible with revised arrangements of protection and main armament. At the 1909 Imperial Conference, and in discussion of Imperial defence, the Admiralty proposed the creation of indigenous fleet units, each to comprise a single Invincible class battlecruiser, three Bristol class light cruisers, and six destroyers. These were to be based in Australia, New Zealand, Canada and South Africa in attempt to secure the naval defence of the Dominions while the Royal Navy concentrated in home waters to meet the German threat. While the scheme was rejected by Canada and South Africa, Australia and New Zealand subscribed, each ordering, and paying for, a modified version of *Indefatigable*, rather than the originally proposed Invincible class. *Australia,* built by John Brown, Clydeside, became a ship of the newly formed Royal Australian Navy, while *New Zealand* built by Fairfield, was presented to the Royal Navy by New Zealand and, in the main, retained and operated in European waters.

HMS Indefatigable (1909)

The Indefatigable class were formally known as armoured cruisers until 1911 when they were redesignated as battlecruisers by an Admiralty order of 24 November 1911. Unofficially a number of designations were used until then, including cruiser-battleship, dreadnought cruiser and battlecruiser.

(Ken Kelly Collection)

HMS Lion (1910)

The 'Splendid Cats', as the class was nicknamed, enjoyed a great reputation within the Royal Navy, though the loss of Queen Mary and the serious damage sustained by Princess Royal at Jutland caused misgivings about the battlecruiser concept.

(Syd Goodman Collection)

LION

Lion Class Battlecruiser

Displacement: 26,350 tons **Dimensions**: 660 ft x 88 ft 6 in x 28 ft **Speed:** 28 knots **Complement:** 1,000 **Armament:** 8 x 13.5-inch, 16 x 4-inch, 2 x 21-inch Torpedo Tubes

Laid Down: 29 November 1909 **Launched:** 6 August 1910

Before commissioning on 4 June, 1912 she underwent important structural alterations; a round funnel was substituted for the original almost oblong foremost one; the height of the other two was increased; a single mast was fitted instead of a tripod.

1913	Flagship of Rear Admiral Commanding First Battlecruiser Squadron.
1914	June, visited Russian ports in the Baltic.
	28 August, present at the Battle of Heligoland Bight.
1915	25 January, took part in the Battle of Dogger Bank; badly damaged, she was towed to Rosyth by *Indomitable*.
	Repaired at Newcastle.
	7 April, rejoined the battlecruisers at Rosyth.
1916	31 May, at Jutland where she was saved from destruction by the heroism of a turret officer, Major F.J.W. Harvey, R.M.L.I. He ordered a magazine to be flooded. He was awarded a posthumous Victoria Cross. *Lion* suffered 101 men killed in the battle.
1919	March, became Flagship of Vice Admiral Sir Roger Keyes, whose squadron guarded the surrendered German Fleet at Scapa.
1920	31 March, reduced to Reserve at Rosyth.
1924	31 January, sold to Hughes Bolckow. Broken up at Jarrow.

The three ships of the Lion class, *Lion*, *Queen Mary* and *Princess Royal*, were significant improvements over their predecessors of the Indefatigable class in terms of speed, armament and armour. They were 2 knots faster, carried 13.5-inch guns in lieu of the 12-inch fitted to the Invincibles, and had a 9-inch thick waterline belt vice the earlier ships 6-inch belt. The ships were built in response to the large German Moltke class battle cruisers, and when completed, the Lion class became the largest warships in the world.

CENTURION

King George V Class Battleship

Displacement: 23,000 tons **Dimensions**: 555 ft x 89 ft x 27 ft 6 in **Speed:** 21 knots **Complement:** 820 **Armament:** 10 x 13.5-inch, 16 x 4-inch, 4 x 3-pdr, 3 x Torpedo Tubes (2 on the beam, 1 in the stern which was removed in 1914-18 war)

Laid Down: 16 January 1911 **Launched:** 18 November 1911

1912	10 December, during speed trials she collided with, and sank, the Italian SS *Derna*.
1913	22 May, commissioned to join the Second Battle Squadron.
1916	31 May, at Battle of Jutland.
1919-23	Spent two commissions in the Mediterranean.
1924	April, became Flagship of Flag Officer Commanding Reserve Fleet (FOCRF) at Portsmouth.
1926-7	Converted at Chatham to a wireless controlled target ship.
1932	Laid up for economy reasons.
1933	Brought into service for gunnery training both at home and in the Mediterranean.
1941	April, converted at Devonport into an imitation of the battleship *Anson*.
	Sailed to Alexandria via the Cape. Her intended use as a block-ship at Tripoli was cancelled.
1942	May, at Aden where she was re-armed with A.A. weapons.
	June, hit by a bomb whilst escorting a convoy to Malta.
	Served as a floating A.A. battery south of the Suez Canal.
1944	March, ran aground at Alexandria; needed docking for repairs.
	12 May, returned to Devonport.
	9 June, was sunk as a blockship off Omaha beach during the Normandy landings.

One of four King George V class battleships, they were criticised for their inadequate secondary armament. Previous ships had carried anything from 4.7-inch to 6-inch and indeed, at the time 4.7-inch was the smallest carried by any of her contemporaries. However, the King George V class mounted only 4-inch guns in their secondary battery, the smaller calibre believed to be a matter of finance. With the signing of the Washington Naval Treaty *Centurion* was decommissioned and had her armament removed. She was converted to operate as a radio-controlled target ship for gunfire up to 8-inch calibre, operating with the Fleet Target Service until 1941. She was controlled by the destroyer *Shikari* which had been fitted with a large deckhouse for the radio-control equipment between the ship's funnels. In 1941 *Centurion* returned to Devonport where she was given a wooden superstructure to create the appearance of being the new battleship *HMS Anson* *(see page 170)*. In this role she deployed to the Mediterranean and took part in Operation Vigorous, giving the impression that the convoy had a battleship escort. She remained off Suez as an AA ship and continued to give the impression that there were more battleships in the area than was really the case. In 1944 she returned to the UK and was one of many ships sunk as blockships to create artificial breakwaters off the Normandy beaches during the D-Day landings in June 1944.

HMS Centurion (1911)

HMS Centurion seen entering Malta. The cutaway in the deck forward of the funnels created a low freeboard aft and this made these ships very wet in any sort of rising sea.

(*Syd Goodman Collection*)

HMS Marlborough (1912)

HMS Marlborough at anchor with awnings spread. Note the secondary 6-inch armament in casemates, arranged so as to give concentration of fire ahead.

(*Ken Kelly Collection*)

MARLBOROUGH

Iron Duke Class Battleship

Displacement: 25,000 tons **Dimensions**: 580 ft x 90 ft x 28 ft 6 in **Speed:** 21 knots **Complement:** 940 **Armament:** 10 x 13.5-inch, 12 x 6-inch, 2 x 3-inch AA, 4 x 3-pdr, 4 x 21-inch Torpedo Tubes

Laid Down: 25 January 1912 **Launched:** 24 October 1912

One of the last of the coal-burning British battleships.

1914	16 June, commissioned to become Flagship of First Battle Squadron.
1916	31 May, at Battle of Jutland. Scored hits on German warships, but she herself was hit by a torpedo thought to have been fired from the *Wiesbaden*. She was escorted back to the Humber. She rejoined the Grand Fleet on 29 July.
1919	12 March, recommissioned for the Mediterranean.
	April, embarked at Yalta, members of the Russian Imperial family escaping from the Bolsheviks.
	May-June, off Theodosia, where she bombarded Bolshevik positions.
1920	March-April and again in June, she landed seamen and marines to occupy points of vantage in Constantinople.
	1 November, paid off at Devonport into the charge of a Care & Maintenance Party. Underwent a long refit when a mainmast was added.
1922	24 January, commissioned for further service in the Dardanelles and off Constantinople.
1924	August, ordered to Alexandria.
	20 September, returned to Devonport; then to Spithead and Sheerness where she recommissioned for further service in the Mediterranean with the Fourth Battle Squadron which later became the Third Battle Squadron.
1926-31	Training duties with the Atlantic Fleet.
1931	April, withdrawn from service. That summer she was used for a series of explosive tests carried out in Plymouth Sound. Gradually increasing amounts of cordite were exploded in her forward magazine. The last one caused damage necessitating docking.
	16 September, sailed to Portsmouth for further tests.
1932	In the Solent, she was used for experiments in bombing from aircraft.
	20 June, left Portsmouth for Rosyth to be broken up by Metal Industries.

An enlarged version of the King George V class, the Iron Dukes were some 2,000 tons heavier and 25 feet longer. Their secondary armament was increased to 6-inch, arranged in casemates although their increase in punch over the earlier 4-inch of the King George V was somewhat mitigated by the fact that they were difficult to fight efficiently in a seaway. Despite this, these ships were highly regarded and considered to have been among the most successful battleship class built for the Royal Navy.

CAROL

RFA Oil Carrier

Displacement: 1,810 tons **Dimensions:** 200 ft x 34 ft x 12ft; **Speed:** 8 knots

Laid down: 14 November 1912 **Launched:** 5 July 1913.

One of the first oil carriers to have her engines and boilers almost right aft.

1914-20	Harbour duties at Devonport.
1920	At Sheerness.
1921	At Portland, operating under Yard Craft agreement.
1925	Returned to Devonport.
1928	In Reserve at Rosyth.
1935	28 June, sold for £2,722 to R.W. McLellan Ltd., and broken up at Bo'ness in August.

AURORA

Arethusa Class Light Cruiser

Displacement: 3,512 tons **Dimensions:** 410 ft x 39 ft x 13 ft 6 in **Speed:** 30 knots **Complement:** 270 **Armament:** 2 x 6-inch, 6 x 4-inch, 1 x 4-inch AA, 4 x 21-inch Torpedo Tubes (a pair port and starboard), (later increased to 8).

Laid down: 24 October 1912 **launched:** 30 September 1913

These were the first class in the RN to be entirely oil-fired.

1914	5 September, commissioned for the Harwich Forces, becoming the Leader of the First - and afterwards - the Tenth Destroyer Flotilla.
1915	24 January, was damaged in the Dogger Bank action, by 3 hits from the German Cruiser *Kolberg*. After the action, *Aurora* rammed - and believed sank - a U-boat.
1916	March, with the Fifth Light Cruiser Squadron in the Hoyer seaplane raid.
1917-18	AA armament increased with 2 more 3-inch guns, and an extra pair of 21-inch TT fitted either side of upper deck.
1918	With Seventh Light Cruiser Squadron in Grand Fleet.
1919	In Reserve at Devonport.
1920	Transferred as a gift to the RCN, commissioning into that service on 1 November, but paid off the following year.
1923	May, reduced to a hulk.
1927	August, sold to A.A. Lasseque, of Sorel in the Province of Quebec.

HMS Aurora (1913)

To assist the artisans in the east end of London, the Admiralty placed the order for her machinery with the Thames Iron Works but owing to financial difficulties this decision had to be rescinded and the machinery was finally ordered from Parsons Marine Steam Turbine Co. Ltd, Wallsend-on-Tyne.

(Syd Goodman Collection)

WARSPITE

Queen Elizabeth Class Battleship

Displacement: 29,150 tons **Dimensions**: 600 ft x 90 ft 6 in x 30 ft 8 in **Speed:** 24 knots **Complement:** 950 **Armament:** 8 x 15-inch, 14 x 6-inch, 2 x 3-inch AA, 4 x 3-pdr, 4 x 21-inch Torpedo Tubes

Laid Down: 31 October 1912 **Launched:** 26 November 1913

She was one of the first group of ships in the Royal Navy to mount 15-inch guns.

1915	5 April, commissioned for the Fifth Battle Squadron in the Grand Fleet.
	17 September, ran over Dumbarton Reefs; her outer bottom was damaged; repaired at Smith's Dock, South Shields.
	3 December, collided with her sister ship *Barham;* ordered to Devonport where a new stem piece was fitted.
1916	31 May, at Jutland her rudder jammed. She was so badly damaged by the enemy that she had to withdraw. Returned to Rosyth for docking.
1917	August, collided with the *Valiant*. She was holed and had to be docked again at Rosyth.
1918	Fitted with aircraft launching platform on 'B' and 'X' turrets; embarked 2 Sopwith Strutter aircraft.
1919-24	With First Battle Squadron in the Atlantic Fleet.
1924-26	Major refit at Portsmouth. Fitted with bulges; 2 funnels were trunked in to one; bridge structure re-designed; additional AA. armament fitted; and aircraft platform removed.
1926-27	Flagship in the Mediterranean,
1928	12 July, struck upon an uncharted rock in the Aegean; the damage necessitated return to UK.
1929-30	In the Mediterranean.
1933	21 March, in thick fog off the mouth of the Tagus, she was rammed by the Roumanian steamer *Peles*.
1933-36	Further reconstruction at Portsmouth, when engines and boilers were replaced; thicker deck armour fitted; bridge structure again re-designed; a hangar built to accommodate 2 aircraft; and a catapult fitted.
1937	29 June, commissioned for service as Flagship in the Mediterranean.
1939	October, detached to Halifax, Nova Scotia to escort a convoy of Canadian troops to England.
1940	13 April, with 9 destroyers, steamed into Ofot Fjord to Narvik. Destroyed eight German destroyers. Her Walrus aircraft bombed and sank *U-64*.
	July, in the Mediterranean, in action with the Italian battle fleet off Calabria.
1941	March, in the Battle of Matapan, damaged two Italian cruisers.
	22 May, damaged by a bomb when off Crete. Repaired in Bremerton Navy Yard, near Seattle, USA.
1942	January, sailed to Trincomalee to become Flagship of C-in-C, Eastern Fleet.
1943	Recalled to the Mediterranean for the invasion of Sicily and the landings in Italy.
	September, led the force which shepherded the surrendered Italian Fleet into Malta. Later, whilst bombarding Salerno she was hit by two radio-controlled bombs which penetrated bottom of the ship. Towed to Malta, then to Gibraltar. Temporarily repaired to enable voyage to U.K.
1944	June, before repairs had been completed, she carried out bombarding duties during the Normandy landings.
	13 June on passage from Portsmouth to Rosyth was damaged by a mine.
	July, returned to the coast of France.

	November, supported the landings at Walcheren.
1945	Reduced to Reserve at Portsmouth.
1946	12 July, sold to Metal Industries Ltd. Her gun mountings and fire-control installations were removed.
1947	April, left under tow for the Clyde. On the 20th the tow parted; she drifted for 3 days; then driven ashore in Prussia Cove.

28 August, wreck sold to a Bristol scrap iron merchant. The job of breaking her up continued until 1956, the task being finally completed by the Wolverhampton Metal Co. Ltd.

HMS Warspite (1913)

Without doubt, the most famous warship ever to leave the slipways of Devonport Yard, she saw service in both World Wars.

(*Ken Kelly Collection*)

HMS Royal Oak (1914)

One of five Royal Sovereign class battleships, *HMS Royal Oak* was sunk on the night of 14 October 1939 while at anchor in Scapa Flow. The German submarine *U-47* had managed to penetrate the anchorage via Hoxa Sound and fired a salvo of torpedos, catching the ship totally unawares. The battleship turned turtle and sank within thirteen minutes, taking 833 of her crew with her. Today, she remains a war grave and in an annual ceremony to mark her loss, Royal Navy divers place a White Ensign on the upturned wreck.

(Ken Kelly Collection)

FEROL

Fleet Attendant Oiler

Displacement: 1,054 gross registered tonnage **Dimensions:** 200 ft x 34 ft x 13ft **Speed:** 8 knots

Laid down: 14 November 1913 **Launched:** 3 October 1914.

First ship with internal combustion engines built at Devonport.

1920	29 January, sold to Anglo-American Oil Co.; renamed *Osage*; re-engined with diesel engines.
1940	18 December, bombed and sunk off Co. Wicklow, Ireland.

ROYAL OAK

Revenge Class Battleship

Displacement: 27,500 tons **Dimensions**: 580 ft x 88 ft 6 in x 29 ft 3 in **Speed:** 20½ knots **Complement:** 908 **Armament:** 8 x 15-inch, 14 x 6-inch, 2 x 3-inch AA, 4 x 3-pdr, 4 x 21-inch Torpedo Tubes (submerged; later removed)

Laid Down: 15 January 1914 **Launched:** 17 November 1914

Originally designed to burn coal, but during construction an 'all oil fuel' policy was adopted.

1916	1 May, commissioned to form one of the Fourth Battle Squadron at Jutland.
1917-18	With the Grand Fleet.
1919-22	Served with the Atlantic Fleet.
1922-23	Eighteen months refit at Portsmouth.
1924	29 April, recommissioned into the Second Battle Squadron of the Atlantic Fleet.
1926	March, transferred to the Mediterranean Fleet, where she spent the next 8 years, returning home to recommission on 1 April, 1927 at Devonport, 27 November, 1929 at Portsmouth and 22 June, 1932 again at Devonport.
1928	Most publicised court martial of the century took place after incidents at a ball on board on 12 January.
1934-36	Paid off into Dockyard control at Devonport for extensive refit.
1936	21 August, commissioned into Second Battle Squadron of Home Fleet.
1937	February, a Spanish aircraft dropped bombs in her vicinity when she was mistaken for the French cruiser *Canarias*. Later an A.A. projectile exploded on her quarter deck.
1938	November, conveyed from Portsmouth to Oslo the body of the late Queen Maud of Norway.
1939	7 June, commissioned for 2½ years service in the Mediterranean, but events in Europe caused her to be re-deployed to Scapa Flow. 14 October, was torpedoed and sunk by *U-47* which had penetrated the defences of Scapa Flow. She sank with great loss of life.

RESISTANCE

Royal Sovereign Class Battleship

Was included in 1914-15 programme but was never commenced. At the outbreak of war, work on warships that could not be completed within 6 months was suspended. Optimistically it was thought the war would end within 6 months. *Resistance* was cancelled on 26 August, 1914.

CLEOPATRA

Caroline Class Light Cruiser.

Displacement: 3,750 tons **Dimensions**: 420 ft x 41 ft 6 in x 14 ft 8 in **Speed:** 28½ knots **Complement:** 301 **Armament:** 2 x 6-inch, 8 x 4-inch, 1 x 13-pdr HA, 4 x 21-inch Torpedo Tubes (in twin mounts amidships; additional pair fitted each side of upper deck in 1916)

Laid Down: 26 February 1914 **Launched:** 14 January 1915

She was fitted with a flying-off platform over the forecastle and one seaplane; but platform was removed in 1916.

1915	June, joined the Harwich Forces.
	August, amongst the force which cut off the retreat into the Bight of the German minelayer *Meteor*, who then scuttled herself.
1916	25 March, in the raid on the Zeppelin station at Hoyer she rammed and sank the German TBD *G194*; she herself was slightly damaged in collision with *Undaunted*.
	4 August, struck a floating British mine off Dunkirk.
1917-18	Remained with the Fifth Light Cruiser Squadron until the end of the war.
1919-20	With the Baltic Force under Rear Admiral Sir Walter Cowan.
1922	April, joined Reserve Fleet at the Nore.
1923-24	After refit at Pembroke, she joined the Third Light Cruiser Squadron in the Mediterranean.
1925	January, joined Second Cruiser Squadron of Atlantic Fleet.
1927-28	Refit at Chatham, then into Reserve Fleet, Nore.
1928	Trooping to Mediterranean.
1928	Trooping to China.
1929-31	Senior Officer's ship of Reserve Fleet, Sheerness.
1931	26 June, sold to Hughes Bolckow Ltd., and broken up at Blyth, Northumberland.

HMS Cleopatra (1915)

A development of the earlier Arethusa class, *HMS Cleopatra* was armed, primarily, with two 6-inch and four 4-inch guns. Both of the 6-inch guns were mounted aft, one superfiring over the other as seen here.

(*T. Ferrers-Walker Collection*)

Submarine J5 (1915)

Seen following transfer to the Royal Australian Navy, the submarine has had a more 'boatlike' bow added with the casing being extended forward and faired into a flared bow.

(Allan C. Green courtesy of the State Library of Victoria)

J5

'J' Class Submarine

Displacement: 1,210 tons (surfaced), 1,820 tons (dived) **Dimensions:** 270 ft x 23 ft 6 in **Speed:** 19½ knots (surfaced), 9½ knots (dived) **Complement:** 44
Armament: 1 x 4-inch, 6 x 18-inch Torpedo Tubes (4 bow, 2 beam).

Laid down: 26 April 1915 **Launched:** 9 September 1915.

1917	Attached to the submarine depot ship *Titania* at Blyth, commanded by Cdr. Edward C. Boyle, VC.
1919	28 January, offered to the Royal Australian Navy. Accepted on 8 February.
1919-22	Attached to depot ship *Platypus*, whose Commanding Officer was Captain E.C. Boyle, VC.
1922	12 July, paid off into Reserve at Westernport.
1924	26 February, sold to Melbourne Salvage Syndicate.
1926	4 June, hull of *J5* was scuttled 3 miles off Barwon Heads.

J6

'J' Class Submarine

Displacement: 1,210 tons (surfaced), 1,820 tons (dived) **Dimensions:** 270 ft x 23 ft 6 in **Speed:** 19½ knots (surfaced), 9½ knots (dived) **Complement:** 44
Armament: 1 x 4-inch, 6 x 18-inch Torpedo Tubes (4 bow, 2 beam).

Laid down: 26 April 1915 **Launched:** 9 September 1915 (along with *J5*)

1916	25 January, Cdr. Max K. Horton was appointed her Commanding Officer to supervise her building and for the first 18 months.
1917-18	Patrolling in the North Sea.
1918	15 October, soon after leaving Blyth, she was sunk in error by the British 'Q' ship *Cymric*. Fourteen men were killed or drowned. It transpired that the *Cymric* had mistaken *J6* on the conning tower to be *U6*.

Both laid down on the same day these were the first locally built submarines. They were laid down on No.5 slip which was still covered, thereby screening the submarines from view. They were launched within five months in the presence of Their Majesties King George V and Queen Mary. Immediately prior to their launching, Their Majesties had watched the bending of the first frame, after it had been drawn from the hot furnace, for one of the next pair of submarines to be built.

K6

'K' Class Submarine

Displacement: 1,883 tons (surfaced), 2,565 tons (dived) **Dimensions:** 338 ft x 26 ft 8 in **Speed:** 24 knots (surfaced), 9 knots (dived) **Complement:** 50-60
Armament: 2 x 4-inch, 8 x 18-inch Torpedo Tubes (4 bow, 4 stern).

Laid down: 8 November 1915 **Launched:** 31 May 1916 (along with *K7*).

The first time she submerged in a non-tidal basin in the Dockyard *K6* refused to surface. Incident caused much consternation amongst the dockyard workmen. Mr. L. Selley, Inspector of Engine Fitters, was later awarded the OBE.

1917	At Swan Hunter's yard on the Tyne, she was fitted with modified 'Swan' bow and her funnel lengthened to prevent heavy seas flooding the boilers.
1918	31 January, she was one of the 12th Flotilla which left Rosyth and in an ensuing melee, in fog, she collided with *Fearless* and almost cut *K4* in half. *K4* sank with all hands. The incident was known as 'The Battle of May Island'.
1919	In Reserve at Rosyth.
1920	In the First Submarine Flotilla at Rosyth; then the Second Submarine Flotilla at Devonport.
1922	Based at Chatham. Again joined the First Submarine Flotilla.
1925	13 November, reduced to being manned only by a Care & Maintenance Party at Chatham.
1926	13 July, sold to J. Cashmore Ltd., of Newport.

K7

'K' Class Submarine

Displacement: 1,883 tons (surfaced), 2,565 tons (dived) **Dimensions:** 338 ft x 26 ft 8 in **Speed:** 24 knots (surfaced), 9 knots (dived) **Complement:** 50-60
Armament: 2 x 4-inch, 8 x 18-inch Torpedo Tubes (4 bow, 4 stern).

Laid down: 8 November 1915 **Launched:** 31 May 1916

1917	16 June, struck *U-95* with a torpedo which unfortunately failed to explode.
1918	31 January, involved in 'The Battle of May Island'. She was steaming half a mile astern of *K6* when that boat sank *K4*. *K7* avoided *K6* but ran over the bows of the sinking *K4*.
1919	November, prepared for sale at Devonport.
1921	9 December, sold to Fryer, of Sunderland.

Submarine K6 (1916)

The K class were designed as large fast submarines with the endurance and speed to keep up with the battle fleet. To achieve such speed they were powered by steam. In the event this turned out to be the Achilles heel of the design. Admiral Jacky Fisher observed that putting steam engines into submarines would be the most fatal error imaginable. In service they were difficult to dive - the boiler fires had to be extinguished, the funnels stowed and inlets and exhausts sealed. As often quoted, "there were too many damned holes" and as a result it would take at least five minutes to prepare the boat for diving. Of the eighteen built, six were lost through accidents.

(T. Ferrers-Walker Collection)

Submarine J7 (1917)

HM Submarine J7 was different to other boats of her class with her conning tower being placed further aft on the casing superstructure. Her remains can still be seen today at Hampton, Victoria in Australia.

(Syd Goodman Collection)

J7

'J' Class Submarine

Displacement: 1,210 tons (surfaced), 1,760 tons (dived) **Dimensions:** 270 ft x 23 ft 6 in **Speed:** 19½ knots (surfaced), 9½ knots (dived) **Complement:** 44
Armament: 1 x 4-inch, 6 x 18-inch Torpedo Tubes (4 bow, 2 beam).

Laid down: 5 August 1916 **Launched:** 21 February 1917

Her submerged displacement was different to *J5* and *J6*. She had a long superstructure with conning tower at after end - a quite different appearance to other boats in the class.

1919	28 January, offered to the Royal Australian Navy. Accepted on 8 February.
1919-21	Attached to the depot ship *Platypus*.
1922	2 July, paid off at Westernport.
1929	1 November, sold to Morris and Watt Pty., of South Melbourne. Towed to Melbourne where she arrived on 18 December.
1930	After being stripped at Footscray, she was sunk as a breakwater at Hampton, Victoria.

Submarines *K6*, *K7* and *J7* were built on the same slipway as the earlier pair. The 'K' class submarines were, except for experiments in *Swordfish* in 1916-17, the first RN submarines to use steam power for propulsion. The idea resulted from the need for submarines which could maintain their station with the Grand Fleet when cruising. The 'K' boats surpassed all previous designs in both size and speed - 24 knots on the surface and 9 knots submerged. However, the design concept was not deemed a success. The first time *K6* submerged in the basin of the Yard she refused to surface. The Inspector of Engine Fitters traced the fault and made temporary repairs. After an anxious two hours the submarine rose to the surface. The incident caused such consternation amongst the Dockyard workers that several of them refused to dive in her the second time.

WATSON

Modified 'W' Class Destroyer

Displacement: 1,300 tons **Dimensions:** 300 ft x 29 ft 6 in x 9 ft **Armament:** 4 x 4.7-inch, 1 x 3-inch AA, 6 x Torpedo Tubes

Originally planned that *Watson* be built by Fairfields but on 26 November, 1918, the contract was transferred to Devonport. The *Watson* would have been Devonport's one and only destroyer but she was destined never to be completed. When construction was well advanced towards launching, work on her stopped. In September, 1919, work commenced on cutting her up on the slipway and the material used for other purposes.

FROBISHER

Cavendish Class Cruiser

Displacement: 9,860 tons **Dimensions**: 605 ft x 58 ft (65 ft over bulges) x 17 ft 3 in **Speed:** 30½ knots **Complement:** 712 **Armament:** 7 x 7.5-inch, 3 x 4-inch, 4 x 3-pdr (reduced in 1932), 6 x 21-inch Torpedo Tubes (4 above water (removed in 1932) and 2 submerged)

Laid Down: 2 August 1916 **Launched:** 20 March 1920

1924-26	In the Mediterranean with First Light Cruiser Squadron.
1927	At Hong Kong and Shanghai.
1928	The first ever Royal Aircraft Establishment air-operated catapult was installed in her at Devonport.
	February, became Flagship of First Light Cruiser Squadron in the Mediterranean.
1929	September, commissioned for the Second Cruiser Squadron in the Atlantic Fleet.
1930	Reduced to Reserve; became Flagship of Vice-Admiral Commanding Reserve Fleet.
1932	Armament reduced to 6 x 7.5-inch and 2 x 4-inch AA, and the deck torpedo tubes removed. She then became a Cadet Training Cruiser.
1935	Extinguished a fire in an oil tanker *Valverda* and towed her 1,000 miles to Bermuda.
1937	Paid off into Dockyard Control at Devonport. There she was refitted when the 7.5-inch guns were replaced by 6-inch in accordance with Treaty obligations.
1939	2 January, towed to Portsmouth to become Harbour Ship for Cadets Training. At outbreak of war, became operational.
1942	Rendered valuable aid to the French destroyer *Le Triomphant* which had been damaged in a cyclone.
1944	Acted as Depot Ship for the little ships of the Normandy invasion fleet.
	August, damaged by a Dackel - a long range pattern-running torpedo.
1945-47	Cadets' Training Ship until relieved by *Devonshire*.
1947-49	In Reserve at Devonport.
1949	26 March, sold to British Iron & Steel Corporation.
	11 May, arrived Newport to be broken up by J. Cashmore Ltd.

Frobisher was laid down during WWI, the keel plate being laid by Lady Maud Warrender, the wife of the Commander-in-Chief, Plymouth. This class of ship was designed to operate in the Atlantic and as it was thought oil fuel might not be obtainable in distant parts, they were planned with some coal capacity and four small coal-burning boilers that would provide sufficient steam for cruising speed. However, after the Armistice in 1918 work on the ship was delayed and she became practically a 'stand-by' ship for the workmen. She was therefore in hand for a longer period than any other modern warship - the original coal/oil concept was no longer deemed necessary and she was completed as an oil-burner. In 1939 she was serving as a Cadet Training Ship, armed with only a single 4.7-inch gun. At the outbreak of war she was laid up at Portsmouth, but in January 1940 she was moved to Devonport to be re-armed with her original 7.5-inch and 4-inch guns. However, being given only a low priority, the work was not completed until February 1942.

HMS Frobisher (1920)

Seen at anchor during WWII *HMS Frobisher* is seen with radar fitted and a tripod mainmast. She served until 1944 when struck by a torpedo forward.
Following temporary repairs at Chatham, she was converted to a Training Ship at Rosyth.

(Syd Goodman Collection)

RFA Olna (1921)

RFA Olna was laid down on the same slip as vacated by *Frobisher* five weeks earlier. Her construction was an economic test and comparison with mercantile shipbuilding firms.

(Syd Goodman Collection)

OLNA

Royal Fleet Auxiliary Oiler

Displacement: 7,023 GRT **Dimensions:** 442 ft x 57ft x 33 ft

Laid down: 14 June 1920 **Launched:** 21 June 1921.

1921	27 October, after trials, she sailed for London. She was manned by RFA personnel but managed by Messrs. Davies and Newman Ltd. until 1936.
1931	October, whilst anchored in the St. Lawrence River, Canada, she was struck by the Newcastle steamship *Cairnross*.
1929	Used for experiments with the Oertz rudder, a streamlined rudder behind a fixed streamlined skeg. By maintaining a better aerofoil shape at all angles it was designed to experience less drag and less rudder torque and help keep single screw ships on a more straight course.
	29 July, took *SS Vimeria* in tow after she had hit an iceberg off the Grand Banks. The tow covered 700 miles and lasted five days.
1937	November, transferred to Admiralty management and manning as an RFA.
1938	November, undertook trials with bow protection paravanes.
1939	Ran aground in Ceylon whilst on passage to Trincomalee, to where she was towed by the cruiser *Manchester*. Her repairs at Bombay took several months.
1940	October, together with *RFA Brambleleaf* established a refuelling base at Suda Bay, Crete.
1941	18 May, she was bombed and set on fire at Suda Bay, Crete by German aircraft; became a total loss.

Built in accordance with the Colwyn Committee's recommendation that surplus facilities of the Royal Dockyards should be used in the construction of merchant vessels. The contract for a second oiler, a fixed price contract, was signed in August 1920, to build *Nassa* for the Anglo-Saxon Petroleum Co. Ltd., of London. This 5,860 ton vessel was laid down on 8 March 1921 and launched on 28 March 1922. She was transferred to her owners on 15 July 1922.

ADVENTURE

Cruiser Minelayer

Displacement: 6,740 tons **Dimensions**: 500 ft x 59 ft x19 ft 3 in **Speed:** 27¾ knots **Complement:** 400 **Armament:** 4 x 4.7-inch, 4 x 3-pdr, 8 x 2-pdr pom-poms (fitted experimentally, removed in 1930), carried around 340 mines

Laid Down: 29 November 1922 **Launched:** 18 June 1924

1927-31	Atlantic Fleet; paid off into Dockyard control 3 November, 1931.
1931-32	Refitted, when original square stern was re-designed to a round one.
1932	3 May, recommissioned with 3/5th complement into Home Fleet.
1933-38	Two separate commissions in China, returning to Devonport for 6 days to recommission in June, 1936.
1939	28 February, reduced to Reserve at Devonport. September, helped lay mine barrage in Straits of Dover. November, struck a mine in the Thames estuary; repaired at Sheerness.
1940	January to August, under refit.
	Helped lay minefield between Orkneys and Iceland; and later in the St. George's Channel area.
1941	16 January, damaged by a mine off Liverpool.
	February to April, under repair.
	July, embarked mines and other stores for passage to Murmansk.
	September to December, at Liverpool for repairs to distorted turbines.
1942	February, damaged in collision whilst leaving the Clyde bound for Murmansk.
	April, rejoined fleet.
	Minelaying operations for remainder of year.
1943	10 April, intercepted, off Cape Finisterre, the blockade runner *Irene*, which scuttled herself.
	May, under repair for machinery defects.
1944	Converted to Repair and Accommodation Ship.
	May, deployed for duty with Allied Naval Commander Expeditionary Force.
	June, deployed off Arromanches in support of Normandy landings,
1945	May, deployed with British naval units at Wilhelmshaven.
	July, paid off into Reserve at Portsmouth and laid up at Falmouth the following month.
1947	10 July, arrived Briton Ferry to be broken up by T.W. Ward, Ltd.

HMS Adventure (1924)

The first minelayer built specifically for the purpose, all others having been adapted from other roles. *HMS Adventure* was built originally with a square stern in which was fitted two large ports through which the mines were dropped. During her first major refit at Devonport the square stern was altered to a round one.

(Naval History & Heritage Command NH64231)

HMS Cornwall (1926)

HMS Cornwall following modernisation. The large box-like structure is the hangar for two seaplanes which replaced the original after superstructure and aircraft arrangements.

(T. Ferrers-Walker Collection)

CORNWALL

County Class Cruiser (Kent Group)

Displacement: 10,900 tons **Dimensions:** 630 ft x 68 ft 3 in x 16 ft 3 in **Speed:** 31½ knots **Complement:** 685 **Armament:** 8 x 8-inch, 4 x 4-inch AA, 4 x 3-pdr, 8 x 21-inch Torpedo Tubes (quadruple mounts; later removed)

Laid Down: 9 October 1924 **Launched:** 11 March 1926

This class comprised the first ships in the RN to be fitted with quadruple torpedo tubes. The proceedings of the launching were 'broadcast by wireless' - the first occasion this had occurred. Funnels lengthened before entering service.

1928-36	Spent three commissions on the China Station with 5th Cruiser Squadron.
1936-37	Extensively reconstructed at Chatham, when AA armament was doubled: a hangar, catapult and 3 aircraft fitted.
1937-39	Used as Boys' Seagoing Training Ship before joining the Second Cruiser Squadron, Home Fleet.
1939	15 March, joined Fifth Cruiser Squadron in China.
1940	Operated in South Atlantic hunting German raiders.
	18 September, with *Delhi*, intercepted French cruiser *Primauguet* and escorted her into Casablanca.
1941	Destroyed the German auxiliary cruiser *HK 33* (renamed *Pinguin*); *Cornwall* was slightly damaged.
1942	5 April, in company with *Dorsetshire*, was sunk off Colombo by Japanese bombers, with the loss of 200 men.

The County class were the first post-war cruisers for the Royal Navy designed within the limits of the Washington Naval Treaty of 1922. In reality the Washington Treaty made no direct mention of Heavy Cruisers, but stated that all warships, aircraft carriers excepted, whose displacement exceeded 10,000 tons standard, or which carried guns of a calibre exceeding 8-inches should be classed as capital ships. In simplistic terms, by default, cruisers could be built up to 10,000 tons and be armed with guns up to 8-inches. With the restrictions on the building of capital ships it fell to the cruiser programmes to provide work for the shipbuilders. With the Royal Navy needing cruisers for trade protection across the vast British Empire and the need to replace ageing cruisers which were facing block obsolescence, the Director of Plans proposed a building programme of eight 10,000 ton cruisers in each of 1924, 1925 and 1926, reducing to four in each of the succeeding years to provide for 28 ships. Following further discussion it was eventually agreed that the 1924/25 programme would comprise five ships which would become the Kent class. The ships were very distinctive with their three slender funnels, which were increased in height by some 15 feet to clear smoke from the bridge works. By the late 1930s *Cornwall*, in common with other ships of the class, was in need of modernisation. Her after superstructure was replaced by a hangar, capable of accommodating two aircraft, and a new athwartships catapult and two cranes for aircraft handling.

DEVONSHIRE

County Class Cruiser (London Group)

Displacement: 9,850 tons **Dimensions**: 633 ft x 66 ft x 167 ft **Speed:** 32 knots **Complement:** 700 **Armament:** 8 x 8-inch, 8 x 4-inch AA, 8 x 21-inch Torpedo Tubes (quadruple mounts). 1 aircraft catapult fitted later

Laid Down: 16 March 1926 **Launched:** 22 October 1927

1929	19 March, commissioned for the First Cruiser Squadron; before sailing, Lord Mildmay of Flete presented to the ship a silver replica of Drake's drum. After several accidents on board, the drum was landed as it was thought to be a jinx.
1931-34	First Cruiser Squadron in the Mediterranean; then Fifth Cruiser Squadron in China; last year in the Mediterranean.
1935	July, at Silver Jubilee Review of the Fleet at Spithead.
1936	Employed in removal of refugees during Spanish Civil War.
1937	May, at Coronation Review of the Fleet at Spithead.
1940	June, conveyed Norwegian Royal family to Scotland.
	7 November, her aircraft assisted *Milford* in destruction of Vichy French submarine *Poncelet*.
	22 November, destroyed German raider *Atlantis* in South Atlantic.
1942	Madagascar operations.
1943-44	May 43-Mar 44, Refit, Liverpool. 'X' turret removed.
1945	June, escorted Norwegian Royal family back to Oslo.
1947	Replaced *Frobisher* as Training Ship for cadets.
1948	Protected British interests at Belize, British Honduras.
1951	Landed parties to protect airport in Grenada during a strike.
1953	At Coronation Review of the Fleet; oldest warship present.
1954	16 June, sold to British Iron & Steel Corporation; broken up by John Cashmore Ltd. at Newport.

NORTHUMBERLAND

10,000 tons County Class cruiser

Early in 1929 Lord Bridgeman, First Lord of the Admiralty, declared that she and her sister ship, *Surrey*, should be laid down without delay. In fact *Northumberland* was to have been laid down as soon as *Exeter* had cleared the slip. However, only preliminary work had been carried out when Mr. Ramsay McDonald announced big 'cuts' in the naval programme. Work on both ships was immediately suspended, and orders cancelled on 1 January, 1930

HMS Devonshire (1927)

HMS Devonshire during WWII service. Compare this image with that of *Cornwall*. Note the lack of a hangar and the more cluttered appearance of the upperdeck due to the addition of numerous close range weapons. At the time of this photograph her single 4-inch guns had been replaced by twin mountings.

(Crown Copyright/MoD 1944)

EXETER

York Class Cruiser

Displacement: 8,390 tons **Dimensions**: 575 ft x 58 ft x 17 ft **Speed:** 32 knots **Complement:** 630 **Armament:** 6 x 8-inch, 4 x 4-inch AA, 4 x 3-pdr, 6 x 21-inch Torpedo Tubes (triple mounts), 2 aircraft, 2 catapults

Laid Down: 1 August 1928 **Launched:** 18 July 1929

1931-33	Second Cruiser Squadron in the Atlantic Fleet.
1933-39	Commodore's ship on America and West Indies Station; returning to Devonport to refit and recommission in July 1936.
1937	June, sent to Trinidad where riots had broken out amongst striking oil workers.
1939	January, with *Ajax*, rendered valuable aid at Concepcion after earthquake in Chile.
	December, Battle of the River Plate when the German pocket battleship *Admiral Graf Spee* was destroyed. *Exeter* badly damaged. Dec 39 - Jan 40, Temporary repairs at Falkland Islands.
1940-41	Refitted at Devonport.
1941	After refit at Devonport joined First Cruiser Squadron in Home Fleet, then to Middle East via the Cape. Afterwards employed on convoy work between Durban and Aden.
1942	1 March, scuttled by her own crew after heroic action against overwhelming Japanese forces in the Dutch East Indies. During action, 54 officers and men were lost, but many more died as prisoners-of-war in Japanese hands.

At the start of World War II, in August 1939, *Exeter's* ships company was recalled from leave and ordered to sail from Devonport within 48 hours. In December, she shared with *Achilles* and *Ajax*, the famous victory over the German pocket battleship *Admiral Graf Spee* at the Battle of the River Plate. The battered cruisers returned triumphantly to their home ports - *Achilles* to New Zealand and *Ajax* to Devonport, where she arrived on 30 January 1940. *HMS Exeter*, which had suffered heavy casualties, first proceeded to the Falkland Islands to carry out temporary repairs to make her fit for the long journey home. She arrived in Plymouth Sound on 15 February 1940 and as the ship went up harbour, Winston Churchill took the salute as she passed the headquarters of the Commander-in-Chief at Mount Wise. Then Churchill, accompanied by Admiral Sir Dudley Pound, First Sea Lord, and Lord and Lady Astor, the Lord Mayor and Lady Mayoress of Plymouth, visited the ship in the Yard. After an extensive refit *Exeter* left Devonport on 24 March 1941 - again in a hurry. She actually left before her refit was complete to avoid the heavy air raids which were then taking place on Plymouth and Devonport.

HMS Exeter (1929)

HMS Exeter, and her sister *York*, shared many of the properties of the County class but mounted only six 8-inch guns in three twin turrets, two forward and one aft. *Exeter* was completed with vertical funnels and masts, vice the raked arrangement in *York*, to make it more difficult for an enemy to calculate the ship's course and speed.

(Ken Kelly Collection)

PENZANCE

Hastings Class Patrol Sloop

Displacement: 1,025 tons **Dimensions**: 250 ft x 34 ft 1 in x 9 ft **Speed:** 16 knots **Complement:** 100 **Armament:** 1 x 4-inch, 1 x 4-inch AA

Laid Down: 29 July 1929 **Floated out of dock:** 10 April 1930

Built alongside *Hastings* in the Shallow Dock, South Yard.

1931	15 January, commissioned for the Middle East. Permanently employed in the Red Sea, only returning to Malta for refits and relaxation of the ship's company.
1933	1 July, recommissioned at Malta.
1935	June, went to the aid of *Hastings* and attempted to haul her off the shore.
	15 September, docked in Khedivial Dock Co.'s yard at Suez.
	29 November, recommissioned at Aden.
1936	July, refitted at Simonstown.
1938	30 March, left Simonstown for Home Waters; joined the Fishery Protection Flotilla.
1939	1 April, commissioned for America and West Indies Station.
1940	24 August, whilst escorting convoy (SC 1) out of Cape Breton Island bound for England, she was sunk by submarine when 700 miles off Irish coast. Ninety of her ship's company were lost.

Before WWI patrol duties on foreign stations had been entrusted to barque-rigged gunboats, sloops and other small vessel of little fighting value and usually ill equipped for the work expected of them. After the war this work was performed by the Flower class sloop, but as they became worn out a different solution was sought. The answer came in the form of a new class of minesweeping sloop specially designed for foreign service and combining the dual role of minesweeper and anti-submarine escort, although in practice their primary minesweeping role was much neglected and focus was placed on escort and ASW work. Although neither one thing nor the other, these sloops did have one point in their favour - they were relatively cheap.

A surprise change in Admiralty policy brought local benefit when the building of two sloops, which had first been allocated to private yards, were re-allocated to Devonport. These sloops, *Hastings* and *Penzance*, were some compensation for the loss of work on *Northumberland*, and helped to dispel the gloom that had been hanging over the Yard concerning its future. They were actually laid down without ceremony at the end of July 1929 in the shallow dock and after being named were floated out on 10 April 1930.

These were the first pair of many other sloops to be launched at Devonport. Most were built in pairs, alongside each other on No.4 slip - *Fowey* and *Bideford*; *Falmouth* and *Weston-super-Mare*; *Grimsby* and *Leith* etc. Only one other ship, *Milford*, was laid down in the shallow dock and she was floated out on 11 June 1932.

HMS Penzance (1930)

She is seen here early in her career with minesweeping davits and a winch on the quarterdeck. Notice the vast array of shrouds supporting the masts, something not dispensed with until the advent of the tripod and lattice mast.

(Ken Kelly Collection)

HMS Hastings (1930)

Compare this WWII image of *Hastings* with the earlier image of *Penzance*. The minesweeping gear has been removed in favour of increased ASW capability, mounting instead depth charge throwers and racks. The Hedgehog AS mortar thrower is mounted right forward just aft of the capstan.

(Crown Copyright/MoD 1942)

HASTINGS

Hastings Class Patrol Sloop

Displacement: 1,025 tons **Dimensions**: 250 ft x 34 ft 1 in x 9 ft **Speed:** 16 knots **Complement:** 100 **Armament:** 1 x 4-inch, 1 x 4-inch AA

Laid Down: 29 July 1929 **Floated out of dock:** 10 April 1930

Laid down alongside *Penzance* in the Shallow Dock, South Yard.

1930-35	East Indies Station; employed in the Red Sea.
1934	11 June, grounded on the Shab Kutb reef, 50 miles from Port Sudan. Badly damaged, necessitating temporary repairs at Suez and permanent repairs at Malta.
1937-38	Captain Fishery Protection and Minesweeping Flotilla.
1939-43	Convoy escort on the East Coast of England; later escorted convoys from Londonderry to Freetown. On the Tyne, her armament was removed and she was fitted out to accommodate midshipmen under training. Attached to Third Submarine Flotilla in Holy Loch, Scotland. Used as target ship for future Submarine Commanding Officers. Later at Londonderry, supervising surrendered German U-boats.
1946	2 April, sold to be broken up at Troon.

FOWEY

Shoreham Class Patrol Sloop

Displacement: 1,105 tons **Dimensions:** 250 ft x 34 ft x 8 ft 6 in **Speed:** 16 knots **Complement:** 100 **Armament:** 2 x 4-inch AA

Laid down: 24 March 1930 **Launched:** 4 November 1930.

1931-39	In the East Indies and Persian Gulf, recommissioning at Colombo on 16 July, 1932 and again on 1 November, 1934.
1940	30 January, along with *Whitshed* and an RAF aircraft of 288 Squadron, she destroyed *U-55* off Ushant.
	29 April, arrived Plymouth after being in collision with one of the vessels she had been escorting.
	20 October, arrived in the Clyde with 157 convoy survivors.
1946	October, sold to Chinese owners; renamed *Fowlock*.
1947	4 May, after refit, left Falmouth for Shanghai.
1950	Finally scrapped at Mombasa.

BIDEFORD

Shoreham Class Patrol Sloop

Displacement: 1,105 tons **Dimensions:** 250 ft x 34 ft x 8 ft 6 in **Speed:** 16 knots **Complement:** 100 **Armament:** 2 x 4-inch AA

Laid down: 10 June 1930 **Launched:** 1 April 1931

Also fitted for minesweeping duties.

1931	25 November, commissioned for the Persian Gulf where she spent the next 7 years.
1932	December, refit at Colombo until 17 February 1933.
1934	March-April, refit at Colombo.
1936	July-August, refit at Colombo.
1937	September-November, refit at Bombay.
1938	12 December, recommissioned in Malta following major refit and re-arming.
1939	July, proceeded to China, but returned home on outbreak of war for a refit at Devonport, completing in February 1940.
1940	Whilst evacuating troops from Dunkirk, she was hit by a bomb, suffered many casualties, lost 40ft. of her stern; she was towed to Dover by *HMS Locust*. Repair work completed in April 1941.
1941	April, rejoined Sloop Division at Liverpool.
1942	1 August, rescued the crew of a US Catalina aircraft in the Bay of Biscay.
1943	Under refit at Avonmouth. Type 271 and Type 291 radar fitted.
	April, worked up at Tobermory for escort duty.
	May, rejoined Western Approaches Command for Atlantic convoy escort duties.
	25 August, was attacked by German jet-propelled wireless controlled glider bombs, but suffered only slight damage.
	September, under repair at Londonderry.
1944	Convoy escort duty in the Mediterranean.
1945	January-March, refit at Devonport.
	April, escort duties in SW Approaches.
	July, reduced to reserve and laid up at Milford Haven in August.
1949	14 July, sold and later broken up at Milford Haven.

HMS Bideford (1931)

An early wartime view of *HMS Bideford*. Her original 4-inch (LA) guns have been replaced by HA mountings. During the war she was to receive an additional four 20mm Oerlikons and Type 286 radar, later replaced by the Type 291 set.

(Syd Goodman Collection)

HMS Leander (1931)

She was commissioned into the Royal Navy as *HMS Leander* on 24 March 1933. Along with her sister *Achilles* she served in the New Zealand Division of the Royal Navy. In 1941 the New Zealand Division became the Royal New Zealand Navy and she was commissioned as *HMNZS Leander* in September 1941.

(Allan C. Green courtesy of the State Library of Victoria)

LEANDER

Leander Class Light Cruiser

Displacement: 7,270 tons **Dimensions:** 554 ft 3 in x 55 ft 9 in x 16 ft **Speed:** 32½ knots **Complement:** 570 **Armament:** 8 x 6-inch, 4 x 4-inch AA
8 x 21-inch Torpedo Tubes (quadruple mounts), 1 aircraft, 1 catapult.

Laid down: 8 September 1930 **Launched:** 24 September 1931

She was the first 6-inch gun cruiser built since 1918, and the first single funnelled cruiser in the RN. Her launching ceremony was broadcast nationally.

1933-36	Flagship of Second Cruiser Squadron in the Home Fleet.
1937	January, prepared for 3 years' service with the New Zealand Division.
	May, represented New Zealand at the Coronation Review at Spithead.
1939	In New Zealand waters protecting coastal shipping.
1940	With the Red Sea forces, based on Aden.
	October, in action with four Italian destroyers, one of which was driven ashore and destroyed by bombing.
1941	27 February, intercepted, and fired upon, the Italian auxiliary *Ramb I* who abandoned ship.
	June, in the Mediterranean supporting Australian forces in North Africa advancing along the coast road.
1942	12 February, one of the original Anzac Squadron.
1943	July, operating with US Task Force in the Second Battle of Kula Gulf in the Solomons. She was hit by torpedo and severely damaged, but reached Auckland safely.
1943-45	Extensive refit in USA which was completed on the Tyne.
1945	26 August, returned to the Royal Navy.
1947	With First Cruiser Squadron in the Mediterranean.
1948	Laid up in the River Fal in Cornwall with other derelict vessels.
1949	15 December, sold to Hughes Bolckow & Co. Ltd.
1950	12 January, left Devonport in tow for breaking up at Blyth, Northumberland.

As completed *Leander* proved to be very wet and the boats stowed on the main deck were damaged at sea. To remedy this issue the forecastle plating was extended aft to the funnel and the boat stowage raised a deck.

FALMOUTH

Repeat Shoreham Class Patrol Sloop

Displacement: 1,060 tons **Dimensions:** 250 ft x 34 ft x 8 ft 3 in **Speed:** 16 knots **Complement:** 100 **Armament:** 1 x 4-inch, 1 x 4-inch AA

Laid down: 31 August 1931 **Launched:** 19 April 1932

1932	25 October, commissioned for service as Despatch Vessel in China, recommissioning in Far East on 18 February, 1935 and again on 8 October, 1937.
1940	24 June, depth charged and sank Italian Submarine *Galvani* which had been attacked by gunfire from other warships.
1944	May, ship's landing party helped capture 51 survivors from German submarine *U-852* which, after attack by the RAF, had beached herself in Somaliland.
1946	July, returned to Plymouth from Far East; first return to an English port for 14 years.
1951	April, became Drill Ship for Tyne Division of RNR and was moored alongside Vickers Engineering Works at Elswick, Newcastle-on-Tyne.
1952	Renamed *Calliope*.
1967	When RNR Division moved ashore in June, she was sold to Messrs. Hughes Bolckow Ltd, who broke her up at Blyth.

MILFORD

Repeat Shoreham Class Patrol Vessel.

Displacement: 1,060 tons **Dimensions:** 250 ft x 34 ft x 8 ft 3 in **Speed:** 16 knots **Complement:** 100 **Armament:** 1 x 4-inch, 1 x 4-inch AA

Laid down on blocks in the Shallow Dock, South Yard: September 1931 **Floated out of Dock:** 11 June 1932

1932	20 December, commissioned to replace *Verbena* on the Africa Station.
1934	February, made a special journey with Vice Admiral A.R.G.R. Evans ('Evans of the Broke'), C-in-C, Africa Station into the Antarctic, visiting Bouvet Island. No other British warship had ever penetrated as far as did *Milford*.
1935-37	After recommissioning at Portsmouth, she spent 2 more years in African waters.
1937-39	Again on Africa Station.
1940	July, joined the fleet patrolling off Dakar to prevent French ships falling in to the hands of the Germans.
	7 November, when off Port Gentil in French Gaboon, she was assisted by the Walrus aircraft from *Devonshire* in a bomb and depth charge attack on Vichy French submarine *Poncelet*, which surrendered to *Milford*.
1946-47	RNVR Drill Ship.
1949	3 June, sold, to be broken up by T.W. Ward Ltd. at Hayle in Cornwall.

HMS Milford (1932)

As completed she has a 4-inch HA gun forward and a 4-inch LA mounting aft. This latter gun was replaced in the late 1930s by a second HA mounting. She is wearing the white hull and buff upperworks colours adopted by Royal Navy warships operating in the tropics.

(T. Ferrers-Walker Collection)

HMS Weston (1932)

Note the new bridge compared to the previous image of *HMS Milford*. Type 271 radar is fitted above the bridge and 20mm Oerlikon guns are sited in the bridge wings. Hedgehog is just noticeable to the side of the forward 4-inch HA gun and the mainmast has been deleted, replaced by a small pole mast further aft mounting an HF/DF aerial.

(Crown Copyright/MoD)

WESTON

Repeat Shoreham Class Patrol Vessel

Displacement: 1,060 tons **Dimensions:** 250 ft x 34 ft x 8 ft 3 in **Speed:** 16 knots **Complement:** 100 **Armament:** 1 x 4-inch, 1 x 4-inch AA

Laid down: 7 September 1931 **Launched:** 23 July 1932

1933	21 February, commissioned for the South America Station.
1935	Exchanged stations with *Penzance* serving in the Red Sea.
	August, recommissioned at Gibraltar. Proceeded to Port Sudan.
1936	July, on Red Sea Patrol.
1939	In the Mediterranean but returned to Home Waters soon after outbreak of war.
1940	31 May, off Lowestoft, sank the German submarine *U-13*.
1941	January, transferred to Northern Escort Force for convoy escort work in the Northwest Approaches and North Sea.
	July, Western Approaches Command for Atlantic Escort duty.
1942	Refit at Dundee where she received Type 271 radar.
1943	June, refit at Belfast to receive HF/DF equipment and Hedgehog AS mortar. On completion resumed Atlantic escort task.
1944	March, transferred to 55 EG at Freetown.
	October, refit at HM Dockyard, Bermuda.
1945	May, withdrawn from operational use and paid off into reserve at Portsmouth.
1947	Used in bomb trials off Milford Haven.
	26 April, in final trial, a bomb was exploded in her engine room which almost severed the ship.
	22 May, sold and broken up in Gelliswick Bay by Howells, of Milford Haven.

She was launched on 23rd July 1932 by Lady Addison as the first RN ship to carry the name. It had been intended to name this ship *Weston-Super-Mare*, but that was considered to be too cumbersome so this was changed before launch to *Weston*.

ORION

Leander Class Light Cruiser

Displacement: 7,270 tons **Dimensions:** 554 ft 3 in x 55 ft 9 in x 16 ft **Speed:** 32½ knots **Complement:** 570 **Armament:** 8 x 6-inch, 4 x 4-inch AA 8 x 21-inch Torpedo Tubes (quadruple mounts), 2 aircraft, 1 catapult.

Laid down: 26 September 1931 **Launched:** 24 November 1932

1933	October, during trials, she collided with an Admiralty oiler; required docking for fitting a new propeller.
1934	16 January, commissioned for the Second Cruiser Squadron in the Home Fleet.
1937-39	With Eighth Cruiser Squadron on America and West Indies Station.
1939-40	In the Atlantic on convoy duties.
1940	May, arrived Alexandria to reinforce the Mediterranean Fleet.
	21 June, bombarded Bardia; a week later, with *Neptune* and *Sydney*, was in action with three Italian destroyers, one of which was sunk.
	September, bombarded Dodecanese Islands.
	October, towed the damaged *Liverpool* to Alexandria.
1941	Sank 3 merchantmen in the Straits of Otranto.
	March, at Battle of Matapan, as Flagship.
	April, the evacuation of Greece was conducted from her.
	21 May, was bombed for 7 hours during the defence and evacuation of Greece.
	28 May, in evacuation of Heraklion she was hit by a bomb which struck 'A' and 'B' turrets, and another which penetrated the mess decks. Her Commanding Officer was killed and there were heavy casualties amongst the ship's company and the troops being carried. She returned to Alexandria, then to U.S. Navy Yard at Mare Island for repairs.
1943-44	In the Mediterranean, operating out of Malta and supporting the landings in Sicily and Anzio.
1944	April, returned to UK.
	June, provided supporting bombardment to D-Day landings.
	August, returned to the Mediterranean, provided gun support to the landings in Southern France.
	October, was Flagship at the re-entry of British troops to Piraeus.
1946	5 July, returned to Devonport for refit.
	September, proposed sale to the Royal Netherlands Navy did not materialise.
1948	She was used, along with *Ashanti* and *Ace*, for underwater trials in Loch Striven, Scotland. She survived one of the biggest charges ever fired.
1949	19 July, sold and broken up at Troon by Arnott Young.

HMS Orion (1932)

HMS Orion at anchor in the 1930s, as completed with pole masts. These were later replaced by tripod masts.

(Syd Goodman Collection)

HMS Grimsby (1933)

The Grimsby class were more heavily armed than the earlier sloops, carrying two single 4.7-inch guns, although in this image the after gun had been landed as the vessel was conducting minelaying trials. A smaller 3-inch gun is mounted above a deckhouse forward of the bridge.

(*Syd Goodman Collection*)

GRIMSBY

Grimsby Class Patrol Sloop

Displacement: 990 tons **Dimensions:** 250 ft x 36 ft x 7 ft 6 in **Speed:** 16½ knots **Complement:** 100 **Armament:** 2 x 4.7-inch, 1 x 3-inch AA
(She was later fitted with mines on quarterdeck in place of the after 4.7-inch gun).

Laid down: 23 January 1933 **Launched:** 19 July 1933

1934-39	East of Suez until the outbreak of war; recommissioning at Singapore on 8 October, 1936 and 16 March, 1939.
1940	In the Red Sea forces.
1941	April, she was at the evacuation of Greece when she displayed excellent seamanship, towing the bombed *SS Scottish Prince* into Suda Bay; and *HMS Glenearn* from Suda Bay to Alexandria.
	25 May, whilst operating with the Eastern Mediterranean Fleet off the coast of Libya, she was bombed and sunk off Tobruk.

LEITH

Grimsby Class Patrol Sloop

Displacement: 990 tons **Dimensions:** 250 ft x 36 ft x 7 ft 6 in **Speed:** 16½ knots **Complement:** 100 **Armament:** 2 x 4.7-inch, 1 x 3-inch AA

Laid down: 6 February 1933 **Launched:** 9 September 1933

She differed from *Aberdeen* in that her AA gun was mounted on a shelter deck forward of the bridge, and she had a shorter forecastle deck. Similar to *Wellington.*

1934-39	In New Zealand waters, commissioning at Wellington in December, 1936 and again in July, 1939.
1939-45	When war began she returned to Home Waters and spent most of the war period on convoy duties which took her to the Mediterranean, Newfoundland, Bathurst and around the British Isles.
1946	25 November, sold and converted at Grangemouth to a passenger ship for a Panamanian Company and re-named *Byron*.
1948	At Grangemouth, was bought by the Danish section of the World Friendship Association and re-named *Friendship*.
1949	Taken over by the Royal Danish Navy; re-named *Galathea*; and used as a deep sea exploration vessel.
1955	October, broken up.

LOWESTOFT

Grimsby Class Patrol Sloop

Displacement: 990 tons **Dimensions:** 250 ft x 36 ft x 7 ft 6 in **Speed:** 16½ knots **Complement:** 100 **Armament:** 2 x 4.7-inch, 1 x 3-inch AA
(She was later fitted with mines on quarterdeck in place of the after 4.7-inch gun).

Laid down: 21 August 1933 **Launched:** 11 April 1934

1934	20 November, commissioned to relieve *Bridgewater* on the China Station.
1934-39	On the China Station until the outbreak of war; recommissioning at Singapore on 4 April, 1937.
1942	12 July, collided with the French destroyer, *Leopard*.
1945	Senior Officer's ship of 57th Escort Group.
1946	4 October, sold for conversion to merchant ship under the Panamanian flag; re-named *Miraflores*. Partially converted at Barry, then completed at Dunkirk.
1948	Arrested for debts; she was laid up at Dunkirk.
1955	Sold to Belgian shipbreakers. 5 August, she was towed to Boom, near Antwerp, to be broken up.

WELLINGTON

Grimsby Class Patrol Sloop

Displacement: 990 tons **Dimensions:** 250 ft x 36 ft x 7 ft 6 in **Speed:** 16½ knots **Complement:** 100 **Armament:** 2 x 4.7-inch, 1 x 3-inch AA

Laid down: 25 September 1933 **Launched:** 29 May 1934

1935	22 January, commissioned for the New Zealand Station.
1937	26 August, commissioned at her name port in New Zealand; served in that area until outbreak of war.
1939	September, temporarily attached to China Station. 5 November, to Freetown for escort duty in North Atlantic, afterwards coastal convoys around the British Isles.
1940	June, took part in 'Operation Cycle', when British troops were evacuated from Le Havre.
1942	November, in 'Operation Torch' - the landings in North Africa.
1943	The 3-inch AA gun was changed for 6 x 20mm Oerlikons. July, on convoy duties off Freetown.
1944	May-July, refit period at Bermuda.
1945	January, attached to Gibraltar Escort Force. After VE-Day, she was employed locating surrendered U-boats. 9 August, paid off into Reserve; laid up at Milford Haven.
1947	25 June, purchased by the Hon. Company of Master Mariners for use as their London Headquarters. She was fitted out at HM Dockyard, Chatham and was moored - where she still lies (2016) - in the Thames alongside Victoria Embankment.

HMS Lowestoft (1934)

HMS Lowestoft as completed. From completion of build in 1934, through to the start of WWII, *Lowestoft* had served exclusively on the China Station, having not returned to the UK for refit. In 1939 she was taken in hand for a refit at Hong Kong where she was fitted with twin 4-inch gun mountings.

(Ken Kelly Collection)

HMS Apollo (1934)

HMS Apollo seen shortly after her launch into the Hamoaze on 9 October 1934.

(*Oscar Parkes Collection*)

APOLLO

Amphion Class Light Cruiser

Displacement: 6,980 tons **Dimensions:** 555 ft x 56 ft 8 in x 15 ft 8 in **Speed:** 32½ knots **Complement:** 550 **Armament:** 8 x 6-inch, 4 x 4-inch AA, 4 x 3-pdr, 8 x 21-inch Torpedo Tubes (quadruple mounts), 2 aircraft with athwartship catapult

Laid down: 15 August 1933 **Launched:** 9 October 1934.

Chief difference to Leander class was arrangement of machinery spaces necessitating two funnels.

1936	7 January, commissioned for America and West Indies Station; travelled 1,000 miles up the Amazon.
1938	11 May, arrived Devonport, conveying the body of the late Mr. J. Ramsay Macdonald, the British ex-Premier.
1938	After refit, was acquired by the RAN, who commissioned her on 29 September, and renamed her *Hobart* on 14 October.
1939	Escort and patrol duties between India and Aden.
1940	August, was at the evacuation of British Somaliland.
1941	Replaced *HMAS Perth* in the Mediterranean.
1942	January-February, heavily bombed when in Malayan waters, but suffered only slight damage.
	6 September, slightly damaged when in collision with a US ship. Returned to Sydney, N.S.W. for repairs.
1943	20 July, torpedoed by a Japanese submarine, receiving considerable structural damage.
1945	April, present at the landings at Tarakan in Borneo.
	31 August, was present in Tokyo Bay for the surrender of the Japanese forces.
1947	August, paid off into Reserve at Sydney.
1953	Commenced 3 years conversion at Newcastle, N.S.W., for use as a Training Ship; but the plan was abandoned before completion.
1962	February, sold to Mitsui and Co. (Aust.) Pty. Ltd.
	3 March, left Sydney for Japan to be broken up.

The Amphion class were a development of the earlier Leander class, the chief difference being in the boiler spacing. The earlier Leanders had their boilers grouped in one compartment amidships which allowed the uptakes to be brought together into one streamlined funnel. While this arrangement was economical on deck space and protection it did expose all of the boilers to flooding in the event of waterline damage amidships. The Amphion class reverted to a more traditional two funnel arrangement with engine and boiler rooms being placed alternately to minimise the risk of all boilers being flooded at one time.

HMAS Hobart (1934)

Despite having similar dimensions to the earlier Leander class, the Amphion class appeared much longer by virtue of their widely separated funnels.

(Allan C. Green courtesy of the State Library of Victoria)

LONDONDERRY

Grimsby Class Patrol Sloop

Displacement: 990 tons **Dimensions:** 250 ft x 36 ft x 7 ft 6 in **Speed:** 16½ knots **Complement:** 100 **Armament:** 2 x 4.7-inch, 1 x 3-inch AA

Laid down: 11 June 1934 **Launched:** 16 January 1935

1935	17 September, first commissioned for the Mediterranean; spent some weeks as Guardship at Suez.
1936-37	July, with *Weston*, formed the Red Sea patrol.
1938	Transferred to the Africa Station to relieve *Penzance*.
	May, docked for overhaul at Simonstown.
1939	March-June, refitting at Simonstown.
1946	In Reserve at Devonport.
1948	8 March, sold to Rees of Llanelly, where she arrived on 8 June to be broken up.

ABERDEEN

Grimsby Class Patrol Sloop

Displacement: 1,060 tons **Dimensions:** 250 ft x 36 ft x 7 ft 6 in **Speed:** 16½ knots **Complement:** 100 **Armament:** 2 x 4-inch AA, 4 x 3-pdr

Laid down: 12 June 1935 **Launched:** 22 January 1936

1936	October, relieved *Bryony* in First Submarine Flotilla in the Mediterranean.
1938-39	Attached to the Mediterranean Fleet as Escort Vessel; one gun had been removed to provide additional accommodation.
1939	August, surveyed anchorages in Southern Greece which could be used by oil tankers in the event of war.
1946	16 December, arrived Devonport after being towed home by tugs *Mediator* and *Storm King*; tow had parted in heavy seas and ships had had to shelter in Corunna.
1949	18 January, arrived Hayle in Cornwall to be broken up.

HMS Aberdeen was selected to complete as a Despatch Vessel to serve as an alternate flagship on the Mediterranean Station. Accordingly she was fitted with extra accommodation comprising an additional deckhouse which extended over the quarterdeck in lieu of the after armament and minesweeping gear. It was intended that the ship be re-armed, but the international situation in 1939 precluded this and she retained her single 4-inch HA mountings although she did acquire a third mounting aft.

FLEETWOOD

Grimsby Class Patrol Sloop

Displacement: 1,060 tons **Dimensions:** 250 ft x 36 ft x 7 ft 6 in **Speed:** 16½ knots **Complement:** 100 **Armament:** 4 x 4-inch (twin mounts)

Laid down: 14 August 1933 **Launched:** 24 March 1936

Similar to *Aberdeen* but differently armed.

1936-37	Escort Vessel in Home Fleet and for 18 months was engaged on special trials.
1938-39	East Indies Station, relieved the *Londonderry* in the Red Sea.

During WWII she acted at various times as an escort vessel, patrol ship and a fleet minesweeper.

1940	Took part in the Norwegian campaign.
1941	Deployed to Londonderry for Atlantic escort duties.
	June, transferred to Newfoundland Escort Force.
	August, refit at Middlesbrough. Fitted with three 20mm Oerlikons and Type 286 radar.
1942	2 June, damaged in collision with tanker *Oil Reliance*. Passage to Liverpool for refit and repair.
	September, rejoined convoy escort duties at Freetown
1943	11 May, combined with RAF aircraft of 58 Squadron in the destruction of *U-528* south west of Ireland.
	1 November, with *Active* and *Witherington* and RAF aircraft of 179 Squadron, destroyed *U-340* off Tangiers.
	17 November, sustained serious damage in collision with US Navy *PC-473*. Taken in hand for repair at Gibraltar.
1944	April, on completion of post refit trials tasked with convoy escort duties in Mediterranean.
	December, returned to UK.
1945	January, escort operations in English Channel and SW Approaches.
	August, Arrived at Hartlepool and laid up in reserve.
1947	Disarmed and fitted as a Radio Trials Ship.
1950	Refitted and a partial hull reconstruction to fit her for further service.
1958	December, paid off into Reserve at Portsmouth.
1959	Sold to C.W. Dorking Ltd. Left Portsmouth on 6 December, in tow for the Tyne to be broken up at Gateshead.

HMS Fleetwood was selected as trials ship for the new dual-purpose 4-inch HA mounting, later to become the standard mounting for all sloops.

HMS Fleetwood (1936)

HMS Fleetwood was selected as a trials platform for a new 4-inch mounting and as such was fitted with two twin dual-purpose 4-inch mountings that were to become the standard fit for future sloops.

(T. Ferrers-Walker Collection)

HMS Birmingham (1936)

A wartime shot of *HMS Birmingham* at anchor in Plymouth Sound. She was unique amongst her sister ships in that she was fitted with a flared bow as opposed to the knuckle bow common amongst RN cruisers of the day reportedly for performance comparisons. As this design was not adopted it can be assumed that the results were not favourable.

(Syd Goodman Collection)

BIRMINGHAM

Southampton Class Cruiser

Displacement: 9,100 tons **Dimensions:** 591 ft 6 in x 61 ft 8 in x 17 ft **Speed:** 32 knots **Complement:** 750 **Armament:** 12 x 6-inch, 8 x 4-inch AA, 6 x 21-inch Torpedo Tubes (triple mounts); 2 aircraft, 1 catapult.

Laid down: 18 July 1935 **Launched:** 1 September 1936.

This class was a development of the Amphion class, with triple, instead of twin, 6-inch turrets.

1937	16 November, commissioned to become Flagship of 5th Cruiser Squadron in China.
1939	Ordered home soon after outbreak of war, to join Home Fleet.
1940	31 March, sailed from Scapa Flow on 'Operation Wilfred' - laying mines in Norwegian territorial waters.
	April, escorted First Expeditionary Force to Norway, and later helped evacuate them.
1941	Escorted troup re-inforcements going to Egypt.
1942	January, sent to the Falkland Islands.
	June, damaged by bomb explosion during 'Operation Vigorous' - a convoy from Alexandria to Malta.
	September, escorted the expeditionary force making a landing in Madagascar.
	November, by a remarkable feat of seamanship she rescued 661 survivors from the B.I.S.N.Co.'s vessel *Tilawa* out of Bombay.
1943	During convoy duties in the Mediterranean she was torpedoed off Derna; badly damaged, she reached Alexandria, and later sailed to the United States for permanent repairs.
1945	9 May, was in Copenhagen for the surrender of the German forces.
1948-49	Flagship of C-in-C, East Indies, until relieved by *Ceylon*.
1950	At Portsmouth, she underwent extensive reconstruction.
1952-53	Took part in later stages of the Korean War.
1955	Flagship of Second in Command, Far East Station, and of Flag Officer Commanding 5th Cruiser Squadron.
1956	In the Mediterranean.
1957-58	Last commission as Flag Officer Flotillas, Home Fleet.
1959	3 December, arrived Devonport to be placed in Reserve.
1960	Sold to T.W. Ward Ltd.
	2 September, left Devonport in tow, to be broken up at Inverkeithing.

The Towns were designed to the constraints imposed by the London Naval Treaty of 1930. The Towns were classed as light cruisers - defined as one having a main armament no greater than 6.1-inch (155 mm) calibre. All three major naval powers, the UK, USA and Japan, sought to circumvent the limitations on heavy cruiser numbers by building light cruisers that were equal in size and effective power to heavy cruisers. Their lack of a heavy calibre gun was compensated for by carrying larger numbers of smaller 6-inch guns - in the case of the Towns four triple turrets.

HEBE

Halcyon Class Minesweeping Sloop

Displacement: 875 tons **Dimensions:** 230 ft x 33 ft 6 in x 7 ft **Speed:** 17 knots **Complement:** 80 **Armament:** 2 x 4-inch

Laid down: 24 March 1936 **Launched:** 28 October 1936.

1937	20 October, commissioned under the Command of the Captain First Minesweeping Flotilla.
1940	June, took part in the Dunkirk evacuation. She embarked about 700 men from the Mole.
1942	June, damaged by Italian cruisers whilst escorting a Malta convoy; later hit a mine but was only slightly damaged and reached Malta safely.
1943	22 November, sunk by a mine laid by *U-453* off Bari on east coast of Italy.

In the early 1930s the Naval Staff were beginning to realise that the twin roles of AS warfare and minesweeping were becoming increasingly incompatible and the larger and more expensive sloops too costly to use in the minesweeping role. The Halcyon class was developed as a smaller, cheaper minesweeping sloop. The class was to comprise 21 vessels built in two groups; the first using reciprocating steam engines, with steam turbines in the latter. Devonport was responsible for the construction of six turbine equipped vessels.

SHARPSHOOTER

Halcyon Class Minesweeping Sloop

Displacement: 875 tons **Dimensions:** 230 ft x 33 ft 6 in x 7 ft **Speed:** 17 knots **Complement:** 80 **Armament:** 2 x 4-inch

Laid down: 7 June 1936 **Launched:** 10 December 1936.

1937	14 December, commissioned into the First Minesweeping Flotilla with which she served until the outbreak of war.
1940	30 May, during the Dunkirk evacuation, she collided with the G.W.R. cross-channel steamer *St Helier*, and was towed 50 miles in to Dover.
1942	24 March, when acting as an escort to QP 9, a homeward bound convoy from Russia, she rammed and sank *U-655*.
1946	Commissioned as a Survey Ship. Went to the Far East surveying the waters around Malaya and Borneo.
1948-52	Based at Lowestoft; surveyed along the east coast of England.
1953	Re-named *Shackleton*; spent the next few years surveying in West of England and Scottish waters.
1961	December, refitted at Devonport; afterwards surveyed the Bristol Channel and Irish Sea areas.
1962	9 November, returned to Plymouth for the last time; placed in Reserve.
1965	Sold to the West of Scotland Shipbreaking Co. Ltd.
	20 November, arrived Troon for breaking up.

HMS Hebe (1936)

A stern view of *HMS Hebe* showing her minesweeping gear on the quarterdeck - the winches, floats and davits clearly visible, as is the after single 4-inch gun.

(Syd Goodman Collection)

HMS Gloucester (1937)

The loss of *HMS Gloucester* was a reminder of how vulnerable warships were to air attack, particularly close in shore and in daylight. Both *Gloucester* and the cruiser *Fiji*, both already low on ammunition following air attacks off Crete, had been sent to support the rescue of survivors from the destroyer *Greyhound*. Having expended most of their ammunition during the attempt they were ordered to rejoin the fleet but were attacked and sunk with great loss of life. Admiral Cunningham reported to the First Sea Lord that, "The sending back of *Gloucester* and *Fiji* to the *Greyhound* was another grave error and cost us those two ships. They were practically out of ammunition but even had they been full up I think they would have gone." Over 1,100 sailors were lost in this one incident.

(Ken Kelly Collection)

LEDA

Halcyon Class Minesweeping Sloop

Displacement: 875 tons **Dimensions:** 230 ft x 33 ft 6 in x 7 ft 3 in **Speed:** 17 knots **Complement:** 80 **Armament:** 2 x 4-inch

Laid down: 16 November 1936 **Launched:** 8 June 1937

1938	17 May, Commissioned for Fishery Protection Service as a tender to *Hastings*.
1939	Joined 5th Minesweeping Flotilla for operations in SW Approaches and east coast.
1940	Relocated to Rosyth for operations in the North Sea.
	May, detached to take part in evacuation of Dunkirk.
	September, with *Saltash* despatched to assist in rescue operations after *Esk*, *Express* and *Ivanhoe* were mined off Texel.
1941	April, transferred to 6th Minesweeping Flotilla based at Harwich.
	August, deployed for local escort of Atlantic convoys based at Stornoway.
	September, nominated for service on Russian convoy routes.
1942	Whilst escorting a homeward bound convoy, from Russia, PQ14, she was torpedoed by *U-435* and sank in the Greenland Sea.

GLOUCESTER

Southampton Class Cruiser

Displacement: 9,400 tons **Dimensions:** 591 ft 6 in x 62 ft 3 in x 17 ft 6 in **Speed:** 32 knots **Complement:** 800 **Armament:** 12 x 6-inch, 8 x 4-inch AA, 6 x 21-inch Torpedo Tubes (triple mounts); 3 aircraft, 1 catapult.

Laid down: 22 September 1936 **Launched:** 19 October 1937

1939	After trials and working-up period in Malta, she proceeded to the East Indies, where she wore the flag of the C-in-C.
1940	May, in the Mediterranean, with four other cruisers, she attacked three Italian destroyers, sinking *Espero*.
	9 July, she was struck by a bomb during heavy air attack from Italian Air Force south of Crete; her Captain and 17 were killed.
1941	11 January, whilst escorting a Malta convoy, she was hit by a bomb which penetrated five decks but fortunately failed to explode. In the same convoy *Southampton* was set on fire, abandoned and sunk by a torpedo from *Gloucester*.
	March, took part in the Battle of Matapan.
	April, bombarded concentrations of enemy transport on the Libyan coast.
	22 May, during intense air attack off south west Crete, she was hit, set on fire and completely disabled. She sank off the Island of Antikithera with very heavy loss of life.

SEAGULL

Halcyon Class Minesweeping Sloop

Displacement: 875 tons **Dimensions:** 230 ft x 33 ft x 7 ft 3 in **Speed:** 17 knots **Complement:** 80 **Armament:** 2 x 4-inch

Laid down: 15 February 1937 **Launched:** 28 October 1937

She was the first all-welded ship built for the Royal Navy

1938	19 July, commissioned in to the First Minesweeping Flotilla at Devonport. Employed in training duties for this hazardous service.
1939	August, Carried out minesweeping trial in Lyme Bay then took up war station at Scapa Flow.
1940	Atlantic convoy defence based at Stornoway.
1941	March, transferred to Harwich.
	September, nominated for service on Russian convoy routes.
1942	2 May, whilst escorting convoy PQ15 bound for Russia, *Seagull* and *St Albans*, manned by the Royal Norwegian Navy, dropped depth charges and forced a submarine to the surface. It proved to be the Polish boat *Jastrzab* (ex-British *P551*) which unfortunately had to be abandoned.
	October, refit during which Type 271 radar was fitted. On completion resumed duties in North Russia.
1943	March, deployed in Home Waters.
	September, return to Kola Inlet.
1944	April, nominated for minesweeping support of 'Operation Neptune', the allied landings in Normandy.
	5 June, sailed from Solent to commence Channel clearance.
	July, to Lowestoft for refit until September.
	September, minesweeping operations off France and Belgium.
1946	Post-war she became a Survey Vessel, surveying off North West Ireland, in the Firth of Clyde, and entrance to the Bristol Channel.
1955	Stricken from the active list, she became a hulk Drill Ship for the Forth Division of RNVR. based at Leith in Scotland.
1956	May, arrived at the yard of Messrs. Demellweek & Redding at Plymouth to be broken up.

HMS Seagull was taken in hand at Rotterdam for the conversion to her new role in September 1945 and two months later went to Chatham for completion of this work, including fitting of Royal Navy specialist hydrographic equipment in HM Dockyard. On completion in April 1946 the ship recommissioned for surveying duties.

HMS Seagull (1937)

Like many of her sisters *HMS Seagull* spent much of her wartime service in Arctic waters. During her time on the Russian convoy routes she helped escort 21 convoys. For work on the Russian convoys many ships were 'Arcticised' during which bow structure was strengthened and additional insulation provided for deckheads and internal bulkheads.

(*Ken Kelly Collection*)

HMS Britomart (1938)

After completing contractor's sea trials in 1939 *HMS Britomart* joined the First Minesweeping Flotilla comprising *HM Ships Bramble*, *Hazard*, *Hebe*, *Sharpshooter*, *Speedy* and *Seagull*. In September 1st MSF took up its war station at Scapa Flow.

(Crown Copyright/MoD 1944)

BRAMBLE

Halcyon Class Minesweeping Sloop

Displacement: 875 tons **Dimensions:** 230 ft x 33 ft 6 in x7 ft 3 in **Speed:** 17 knots **Complement:** 80 **Armament:** 2 x 4-inch

Laid down: 22 November 1937 **Launched:** 12 July 1938

1939	20 June, first commissioned to relieve the *Niger* in the First Minesweeping Flotilla at Portland.
1942	31 December, whilst escorting convoy JW 51B bound for Russia, was detached to search for scattered vessels. She was intercepted by, and sunk in combat with, the German cruiser *Hipper* and three destroyers. Eight officers, including her Commanding Officer, and 113 ratings were lost.

BRITOMART

Halcyon Class Minesweeping Sloop

Displacement: 875 tons **Dimensions:** 230 ft x 33 ft 6 in x 7 ft 3 in **Speed:** 17 knots **Complement:** 80 **Armament:** 2 x 4-inch

Laid down: 1 January 1938 **Launched:** 23 August 1938

Constructed side by side and on same slip as *Bramble*.

1939	22 August, first commissioned.
1944	27 August, was sunk off the French coast, along with *Hussar*, by an Allied air strike which mistook our minesweepers for the enemy. The CO of *Britomart*, 1 other officer and 20 ratings were lost.

The incident resulting in the loss of *Britomart* and *Hussar*, the writing off of *Salamander* due to her damage and damage to *Jason*, *Colsay* and *Lord Ashfield* was a tragedy that should never have happened. The group of ships had been enjoying a day of rest at Arromanches following sweeping duties off the Normandy beaches when they were ordered to sea to clear a passage to enable the battleship *Warspite* and the monitors *Erebus* and *Roberts* to close the shore to engage German positions around Le Havre. Having first checked with the Minesweeping HQ ship *Ambitious* that their change in orders had been notified to the relevant commands, the ships proceeded with their minesweeping task. On the morning of 27 August 1944 Typhoon aircraft from 263 and 266 Squadrons attacked what they had been informed were enemy ships, there being no reports of Allied ships being in the area. At a subsequent enquiry it was established that although the signal changing the ships orders had been sent, one address had been omitted from the information line, that of Flag Officer British Assault Area (FOBAA). As a result FOBAAs staff were unaware that the 1st MSF were operating in the area. Because of that one small omission 12 minutes of air attack by friendly forces resulted in the loss of three ships with three more damaged. The human cost was 78 officers and ratings killed and 149 wounded.

TRINIDAD

Fiji Class Cruiser

Displacement: 8,000 tons **Dimensions:** 538 ft x 62 ft x 16 ft 6 in **Speed:** 33 knots **Complement:** 980 **Armament:** 12 x 6-inch, 8 x 4-inch AA, 6 x 21-inch Torpedo Tubes, 3 aircraft, 1 catapult.

Laid down: 21 April 1938 **Launched:** 14 October 1939.

1941	October, completed but her life was destined to be short.
1942	March, whilst providing close cover to Russian convoys, with destroyers *Fury* and *Eclipse* she was in action with 3 German destroyers, one of which *Z 26* was sunk. *Trinidad* was hit by one of her own torpedoes which, although fired at the enemy, had veered off course. She reached Murmansk and was docked by her own ship's staff. Repairs were completed in May.
	13 May, sailed under escort of 4 destroyers. Next day they suffered heavy bombing and attack from torpedo-carrying aircraft. She was so badly damaged that salvage proved impossible.
	15 May, she was sunk by a torpedo from *HMS Matchless*.

HMS Trinidad survived in service for barely seven months - her fate decided by a variety British of torpedoes. While escorting Convoy PQ-13 in March 1942, she and other escorts were in combat with German Narvik class destroyers. She launched a torpedo attack but one of her torpedoes had a faulty gyro mechanism, possibly affected by the icy waters. The path of the torpedo formed a circular arc, returning and striking *Trinidad* and killing 32 men. The cruiser was towed clear of the action and was eventually able to proceed under her own power towards Murmansk where she underwent repairs. Repairs completed she set out to return to the UK on 13 May 1942, escorted by the destroyers *Foresight*, *Forester*, *Matchless* and *Somali*. Despite repairs the cruiser was only able to cruise at 20 knots and en route, she was attacked by more than twenty Ju-88 bombers on 15 May. She was hit by several bombs in the forward structure which wrecked repair work and caused an outbreak of several fires. The decision was taken to scuttle her and she was sunk by torpedoes fired from the destroyer *Matchless*.

MOORFIRE

Moor Class Mooring Vessel

Displacement: 720 tons **Dimensions:** 135 ft x 30 ft x 11 ft **Speed:** 9 knots **Armament:** 1 x 12-pdr AA, 1 x 20mm AA

Laid down: 28 November 1940 **Launched:** 24 May 1941

1941	30 November, completion date.
1963	26 March, sold to Messrs. J.A. White, St. David's Harbour, Scotland, who broke her up.

HMS Trinidad (1939)

Based on the Southampton class but design displacement was squeezed to 8,000 tons. The transom stern reduced vibration making the after turrets very steady and also improving speed and manoeuvrability. However, they were cramped and uncomfortable ships for a full wartime complement - this was slightly improved once the aviation facilities were removed and the hangars rebuilt to provide extra accommodation.

(Syd Goodman Collection)

HMS Centurion (as Anson) (1941)

HMS Centurion in Plymouth Sound following her conversion at Devonport in 1941 where she was fitted with a false superstructure made of wood and canvas so as to resemble the battleship *HMS Anson*.

(*Syd Goodman Collection*)

WWII ACHIEVEMENTS

Although Devonport continued to build warships throughout WWII the men and women of the Dockyard achieved many remarkable things during the 1939-45 conflict. In addition to the construction of an aircraft carrier, a cruiser and six submarines the dockyard undertook the damage repair and refitting of over 200 destroyers in the first eighteen months of the war. A major technical achievement was the docking and repair of the destroyer *Javelin* whose bow, as far as her bridge, and stern had been blown off following a torpedo attack by the German destroyer *Hans Lody* on the night of 24/25 November 1941 - only 155 feet of her original 353 feet of her hull remained. She was under repair for just four weeks. The Yard carried out the refitting and modernisation of ten battleships and many cruisers. Most of Britain's best known battleships, *King George V*, *Anson* and *Howe* were, at one time or other, in the Yard. Devonport was also responsible for the repairs to the cruisers *Exeter* and *Ajax* in the wake of the Battle of the River Plate. The Yard also accomplished the almost complete reconstruction of the cruiser *Belfast* when, in the Firth of Forth on 21 November 1939, a mine exploded under her starboard side, breaking the ship's back between the bridge structure and her forward funnel. Following a survey at Rosyth, the ship was secretly sailed for Devonport where she was under repair until the end of October 1942. The repair of the cruiser *Kent*, having sustained severe torpedo damage in the Mediterranean in September 1940, also fell to the men and women of Devonport. Whilst in dock during April 1941, she was hit by a bomb from a German aircraft, but it conveniently exploded in the vicinity of the existing damage. She recommissioned to join the Home Fleet at Scapa Flow in October 1941.

Devonport was also assigned some less than ordinary projects. She was tasked to prepare the destroyer *Campbeltown* for an attack on the dock gates at St Nazaire. She was fitted out in Devonport Yard between 10-19 March 1942 when bullet-proof plating was fitted around her bridge and along the deck edges to protect the raiding force; eight 20mm Oerlikon guns replaced her main armament; and torpedo tubes, depth charges and all ammunition were removed. Her after two funnels were also removed and the foremost two cut at an angle so as to give the ship the appearance of a German Mowe class torpedo boat. Explosives were fitted in the bows of the ship.

CENTURION (as ANSON)

King George V Class Battleship

Devonport was also tasked with creating a dummy battleship. *HMS Centurion*, launched at Devonport in 1911, was removed from the effective list of the Navy in 1926 under the terms of the Washington Treaty. On 14 April that year, she paid off into Dockyard Control at Chatham, where she was converted to a wireless controlled Fleet Target ship. In April 1941 she was taken in hand at Devonport to be converted to an imitation of the King George V class battleship *Anson*. The dockyard estimated the work would take a month but it had to be done in two weeks. The work went on day and night, sometimes during heavy air raids. Her after funnel was removed, a dummy one fitted amidships and her fore one raised. Other major items fitted were three gun turrets made of wood and canvas, with wooden cylinders as barrels; a dummy crane and hangar; and a wooden tripod mast. In June 1942, the dummy *Anson* sailed with 'Operation Vigorous' in the eastern Mediterranean to simulate an operational battleship. Between 1942 and 1944 she was stationed off Suez as an anti-aircraft ship and to dissuade the Italian Navy from action in the area - the Italians thought that her false wooden 13.5-inch guns were real and kept their capital ships away.

HMS Thule (1942)

HMS Thule served in the Far East for much of her wartime career, where she sank twenty vessels by gunfire in the Strait of Malacca in a twelve-day period between 17 December to 29 December 1944.

(Crown Copyright/MoD 1946)

TUDOR

'T' Class Patrol Submarine (Group III)

Displacement: 1,090 tons (surfaced), 1,575 tons (dived) **Dimensions:** 275 ft x 26 ft 6 in x 14 ft 9 in **Speed:** 15 knots (surfaced), 9 knots (dived) **Complement:** 68 **Armament:** 1 x 4-inch, 1 x 20mm AA, 11 x 21-inch Torpedo Tubes (8 bow tubes (2 external), 2 external amidships (rear-facing), 1 external tube aft)

Laid down: 20 September 1941 **Launched:** 23 September 1942.

1944	January, completed. First operated off Malaya.
1944-45	Carried out 7 war patrols in Far East, based firstly in Trincomalee and then Fremantle. A total of 14 small enemy vessels were sunk. She also carried out minelaying operations and some special missions landing agents.
1946	Made available to scientists engaged in exploring the sea bed.
	5 August, left Plymouth to carry out exploration off the western coasts of UK.
1950's	During the 1950's she was one of the T' class which, being of riveted construction, were streamlined and not converted as the welded boats were. Her periscope, aerials and bridge were housed in a fin; the guns and external torpedo tubes were removed. This increased her displacement but it produced a higher speed without any increase in engine power and made her more silent under water.
1963	1 July, sold out of the service.
	27 July, arrived Faslane, Scotland to be broken up.

THULE

'T' Class Patrol Submarine (Group III)

Displacement: 1,090 tons (surfaced), 1,575 tons (dived) **Dimensions:** 275 ft x 26 ft 6 in x 14 ft 9 in **Speed:** 15 knots (surfaced), 9 knots (dived) **Complement:** 68 **Armament:** 1 x 4-inch, 1 x 20mm AA, 11 x 21-inch Torpedo Tubes (8 bow tubes (2 external) 2 external amidships (rear-facing), 1 external tube aft)

Laid down: 20 September 1941 **Launched:** 22 October 1942.

1944	Conducted trials in Kilbrennan Sound to find a way to air-condition submarines.
	November-December, operating in the Malacca Strait. She is believed to have sunk a Ro-100 class submarine.
1945	23 March, left Trincomalee having been loaned to the US Forces.
	May, evacuated military personnel from Malaya. Afterwards she returned to Fremantle where she was holed by *Stubborn* when berthing alongside. Arrived Chatham 23 December.
1946	After refit, she commissioned into the Fifth Submarine Flotilla, based first at Portsmouth and later at Portland. Being of riveted construction she was streamlined similarly to *Tudor*.
1960	18 November, damaged when, during exercises in the Channel she surfaced under *RFA Black Ranger*.
1962	14 September, arrived Inverkeithing to be broken up by T.W. Ward.

TOTEM

'T' Class Patrol Submarine (Group III)

Displacement: 1,090 tons (surfaced), 1,575 tons (dived) **Dimensions:** 275 ft x 26 ft 6 in x 14 ft 9 in **Speed:** 15 knots (surfaced), 9 knots (dived) **Complement:** 68 **Armament:** 1 x 4-inch, 1 x 20mm AA, 11 x 21-inch Torpedo Tubes (8 bow tubes (2 external) 2 external amidships (rear-facing), 1 external tube aft)

Laid down: 22 October 1942 **Launched:** 28 September 1943

1945	9 January, completed and joined the British Pacific Fleet.
1950's	During the 1950's at Chatham, she was converted. Being of welded construction, the pressure hull was severed at the engine room section, and a new section 12 feet long built in. The extra space was used to accommodate two extra electric motors. All guns and external torpedo tubes were removed.
1964	November, sold to Israel.
1965	June, commenced refit at Portsmouth prior to transfer.
1967	10 November, commissioned into Israeli Navy. Re-named *Dakar*.
1968	26 January, on passage to Haifa she was lost in the Eastern Mediterranean. No trace of her was found.
1969	February, a distress buoy was found on a beach in the Gaza strip, marked *"Dakar - S.O.S. - finder inform Coastguard or police"*.

The Group III 'T' class submarines were the ultimate development of the type and comprised some 40 submarines, although five were subsequently cancelled and a further four re-ordered as 'A' class submarines. *Tudor* and *Thule* were ordered under the 1941 programme, *Totem* and *Truncheon* under the 1942 programme. The class was the most numerous ocean patrol type built for the Royal Navy and although initially lacking in range and speed and habitability for the Pacific area of operations conversion of No's 3 and 5 main ballast tanks into fuel tanks conferred a reasonable range of 11,000 nm. 'T' class construction was only dropped after it had become increasingly difficult to incorporate all the latest modifications brought about by the necessities of war, and the 'A' class were ready for mass production. Welding gradually replaced riveting and while the first pair of Devonport boats was of partly welded construction both *Totem* and *Truncheon* were completely welded, which gave them an improved rated maximum diving depth of 350 feet.

HMS Totem (1943)

HMS Totem while serving in Australian waters during WWII. Note the stern torpedo tube and the two aft facing amidships tubes - one on each side.

(Allan C. Green courtesy of the State Library of Victoria)

HMS Truncheon (1944)

The reconstructed *HMS Truncheon* shows the extent to which the appearance of the eight reconstructed submarines changed from their original WWII configuration. The submarines now presented a much quieter target as their prey had changed from surface targets to tracking and destroying enemy submarines.

(Syd Goodman Collection)

TRUNCHEON

'T' Class Patrol Submarine (Group III)

Displacement: 1,090 tons (surfaced), 1,575 tons (dived) **Dimensions:** 275 ft x 26 ft 6 in x 14 ft 9 in **Speed:** 15 knots (surfaced), 9 knots (dived)
Complement: 68 **Armament:** 1 x 4-inch, 1 x 20mm AA, 11 x 21-inch Torpedo Tubes (8 bow tubes (2 external) 2 external amidships (rear-facing), 1 external tube aft)

Laid down: 5 November 1942 **Launched:** 22 February 1944

She saw no active service under wartime conditions.

1952	At Chatham, she was converted similarly to *Totem* except that a 20 foot section was built into her.
1962	15 January, arrived Rosyth for refit, and to be re-engined.
1968	9 January, at Gosport, she was handed over to the Israeli Navy to replace the *Dakar* (ex-*Totem*) lost on passage. Re-named *Dolphin*, she arrived in Israel on 31 January.

Eight of the all welded submarines were reconstructed after WWII. The work was carried out in the Royal Dockyards between 1949 and 1956. The pressure hulls were cut in two at the after end of the engine room and lengthened by 20 feet in Truncheon and 14 feet in Totem. The new section contained a second pair of electric motors and a fourth battery compartment. All gun armament was removed and external torpedo tubes taken out with the bows being reshaped. The hull and casing were streamlined and all external fittings were removed or made retractable. The bridge structure was shaped into a large fin which housed periscopes, radar masts snorts and a wireless mast. A small bridge was placed low in front of the fin. The torpedo armament was reduced to just the six internal bow tubes with space for 12 reloads. New sonar and improved search and attack radar sets were introduced. The reconstruction made the boats far more silent under water and their underwater speed almost doubled.

TERRIBLE

Majestic Class Light Fleet Aircraft Carrier

Displacement: 14,000 tons **Dimensions:** 695 ft x 80 ft (112 ft 6 in across Flight Deck) x 21 ft 4 in **Speed:** 24.8 knots **Complement:** 1,100 (including Squadron Personnel) **Armament:** 30 x 40mm **Aircraft:** 39-44.

Laid down: 19 April 1943 **Launched:** 30 September 1944.

She was the only aircraft carrier to have been built and completed in a Royal Dockyard.

1948	16 December, formally handed over to the Royal Australian Navy. Re-named *Sydney*.
1949	5 February, accepted for service. Left Devonport on 12 April, with the 20th Carrier Air Group on board.
1950	July, returned to Portsmouth to embark 21st Carrier Air Group.
1951-53	Saw active service in the Korean War.
1952	She was an observer ship to the atomic bomb explosion at Monte Bello Island.
1953	Attended Coronation Fleet Review at Spithead.
1955	1 May, became a Training Ship until 1958.
1958	22 January, placed in Reserve.
1961-62	Underwent limited conversion.
	7 March, she commissioned as a Fast Transport Vessel for use in the Vietnam War. On withdrawal of Australian troops from the war, she reverted to a Training Ship.
1973	July, announced that she be taken out of service. She remained in Reserve until being sold for 673,000 Australian dollars to Dong Kuk Steel Mill Co. Ltd.
1975	23 December, towed from Sydney for breaking up in South Korea.

POLYPHEMUS

Centaur Class Aircraft Carrier

Displacement: 18,300 tons **Dimensions:** 650 ft x 90 ft

Ordered on 11 August, 1943, but she was never laid down. Cancelled in October, 1945.

As the war neared its conclusion the shipbuilding programme was thrown into disarray as priorities switched to the production of landing craft needed for the Normandy landings and subsequent landings in the Pacific theatre. Machinery contractors were unable to meet the demands of the complete shipbuilding requirements and there were question marks over how the extensive build programme would be manned and indeed whether the ships in the programme would be completed before the end of the war or even needed in a post-war navy. *Polyphemus* was scheduled to be laid down in October 1944 - her machinery had already been ordered, but in March 1944 builders were told to halt work on the Centaur class carriers. *Polyphemus* never made it onto the slip, the contract being cancelled in October 1945.

HMS Terrible (1944)

HMS Terrible is launched into the waters of the Hamoaze on 30 September 1944 by the wife of the British politician Duncan Sandys. Work on the ship continued until the end of WWII, when the Admiralty ordered the suspension of all warship construction.

(*State Library of Victoria*)

HMAS Sydney (ex-Terrible) (1944)

HMAS Sydney at anchor in Plymouth Sound. A commissioning crew for the aircraft carrier was raised in Australia from the ship's company of the decommissioned cruiser *HMAS Hobart*. *Terrible* was handed over to the RAN on 16 December 1948, and was commissioned at 1200 as *HMAS Sydney*. Following work-up in the UK the carrier sailed from Devonport on 12 April 1949, arriving at Jervis Bay, Australia, on 25 May.

(Syd Goodman Collection)

ACE

'A' Class Patrol Submarine

Displacement: 1,120 tons (surfaced), 1,620 tons (dived) **Dimensions:** 279 ft 3 in x 22 ft 3 in x 17 ft **Speed:** 18 knots (surfaced), 8 knots (dived) **Complement:** 60 **Armament:** 1 x 4-inch, 1 x 20mm AA, 10 x 21-inch Torpedo tubes (6 bow and 4 stern; 4 being external)

Laid down: 3 December 1943 **Launched:** 14 March 1945

Completion cancelled

1948-50	Used with *Orion* and *Ashanti* in Loch Striven to test effects of non-contact underwater explosions, with *Ace* both on, and below, the surface. Trials completed in March, 1950.
1950	June, arrived Port Glasgow to be broken up by Messrs. Smith and Houston.

ACHATES

'A' Class Patrol Submarine

Displacement: 1,120 tons (surfaced), 1,620 tons (dived) **Dimensions:** 279 ft 3 in x 22 ft 3 in x 17 ft **Speed:** 18 knots (surfaced), 8 knots (dived) **Complement:** 60 **Armament:** 1 x 4-inch, 1 x 20mm AA, 10 x 21-inch Torpedo tubes (6 bow and 4 stern; 4 being external)

Laid down: 8 March 1944 **Launched:** 20 September 1945

Completion cancelled

1950	May-June, used in hull strength trials conducted off Gibraltar, from *HMS Flamborough Head*.
1950	20 June, was lowered from four lifting craft, L.C. 8, 9, 23 and 24, until hull collapsed. The ruptured hull was lifted and after examination by scientists, was sunk to the eastwards of Gibraltar.

The 'A' class submarines were intended for operations in the Far East, with emphasis on habitability, range and maximum torpedo stowage. With the end of the war only sixteen boats were completed, the remaining thirty on order, or under construction, being cancelled. Both *Ace* and *Achates* had been launched so their hulls were used in a variety of trials before eventually being disposed of.

SALISBURY

Type 61/Salisbury Class Aircraft Direction Frigate

Displacement: 2,170 tons **Dimensions:** 330 ft x 40 ft x 15 ft 6 in **Speed:** 25 knots **Complement:** 224 **Armament:** 2 x 4.5-inch (twin mount), 2 x 40mm AA (twin mount), 1 x Squid AS Mortar

Laid down: 23 January 1952 **Launched:** 25 June 1953.

The first new warship built at Devonport since the Second World War. First all-welded ship to be built on a pre-fabricated principle.

1956	Commissioned for service on Home/Mediterranean/Middle East and Far East Stations.
1961-62	Extended refit at Devonport. Lattice mast replaced.
1963-64	Service East of Suez.
1964	May, returned to UK to join the 23rd Escort Squadron.
	25 June, off the Isle of Wight, she was in collision with the destroyer *Diamond*, and extensively damaged.
1965	East of Suez; involved in Indonesian confrontation.
1967	Stand by duties in Anguilla crisis. Diverted to the assistance of the German tanker *Essberger Chemist*, which, carrying a dangerous cargo, had broken in two. Destroyed by *Salisbury* and the submarine *Dreadnought*.
1967-70	Extended refit. Sea Cat missile system fitted in lieu of twin 40mm.
1974	1 November, commissioned for service East of Suez.
1975	26 August, became the first RN Ship to transit the Suez Canal north-bound after it re-opened.
	She was the last ship to carry out a Beira patrol off Mozambique.
1976	Deployed in the Cod War off Iceland.
1978	June, proposed sale to Egypt fell through. Lay idle at Chatham.
1980	May, towed to Devonport to replace *HMS Ulster* in the River Tamar, as a Training Ship for new-entry recruits at *HMS Raleigh*.
1985	Replaced in training role by the Leander class frigate *HMS Ajax*.
	14 September, towed from Plymouth for use as a target.
	30 September, Sunk 300 miles west of Ireland following attacks by laser-guided bombs dropped from Buccaneer aircraft and a Harpoon missile fired from a Nimrod. The final blow was delivered by a Sub-Harpoon missile fired from the nuclear-powered submarine *HMS Trafalgar*.

HMS Salisbury (1953)

HMS Salisbury seen after her first modernisation, 1961-62. It shows the double-bedstead Type 965P radar on her plated-in mainmast. She still retains her Type 982 aft of the mainmast and a twin 40mm gun which was later replaced by the Sea Cat missile launcher.

(Crown Copyright/MoD)

HMS Plymouth (1959)

HMS Plymouth is seen here prior to her modernisation with original lattice mast and no aviation facilities. There was a single 40mm Bofors on the after superstructure and two triple-barrelled Mk10 Limbo AS mortars in a well deck aft of that.

(Crown Copyright/MoD 1966)

PLYMOUTH

Type 12/Rothesay Class Anti-submarine Frigate

Displacement: 2,600 tons **Dimensions:** 360 ft x 41 ft x 17 ft 3in **Speed:** 30 knots **Complement:** 235 **Armament:** 2 x 4.5-inch (twin mount), 1 x 40mm AA, 2 x Mk10 AS Mortar; 12 x 21-inch AS Torpedo Tubes (four fixed on each beam firing aft and angled at 45°, two twin trainable launchers mounted forward of the fixed tubes, one mounting on each beam). The torpedo tubes were unsuccessful and were removed from all ships by 1963.

Armament following 1966-69 refit: 2 x 4.5-inch (twin mount), Sea Cat missiles (quad launcher), 1 x Mk10 AS Mortar
Aircraft: Wasp helicopter

Laid down: 1 July 1958 **Launched:** 20 July 1959

1961	11 May, commissioned for General Service Commission on Home/East of Suez.
	June, sailed from Devonport as Leader of the 29th Escort Squadron, based at Singapore.
1964-66	Spent 13 months East of Suez.
1966	April. Intercepted the Greek-registered oil tanker *Joanna V* during Beira Patrol.
1966-69	Extensive refit at Chatham. Facilities provided for operating a Wasp helicopter.
1971	Five month refit at Devonport.
1972	July, left Devonport for the West Indies and U.S.A.
1974	Refitted at Gibraltar, under the "Conveyer-belt system."
1975	22 July, left Plymouth for 9 months in Indian Ocean and Far East.
1978	30 May, co-ordinated the destruction of the remains of the Greek tanker *Eleni V* which, 24 days earlier, had been cut in half by a French freighter off the East Anglian coast. 7 September, arrived Chatham for major refit.
1980	October, sea trials.
1981	Captain Sixth Frigate Squadron.
1982	April, exercise Springtrain at Gibraltar. To South Atlantic as part of Task Force to retake Falkland Islands.
1983	Deployed to West Indies and USA until August.
1984	20 January, to West Indies as Senior Ship of the Dartmouth Training Squadron. Returned to UK in April.
1985	April, deployed to Caribbean as West Indies Guard Ship.
	July, refit at Rosyth. Cheverton Motor Boat removed and additional 20mm guns mounted.
1986	Boiler room fire killed two crew.
1987	November, West Indies deployment.
1988	28 April, decommissioned
	Opened to the public for one year at Millbay Dock, Plymouth.
1990	June, bought by the Warship Preservation Trust and towed to Glasgow for public display.
1991	To Cammell Lairds for brief repairs before being placed on public display at Birkenhead.
2006	6 February, Warship Preservation Trust closed citing financial difficulties.
2014	20 August, towed from Birkenhead for recycling in Turkey.

TARTAR

Type 81/Tribal Class General Purpose Frigate

Displacement: 2,300 tons **Dimensions:** 350 ft x 42 ft 3 in x 17 ft 6 in **Speed:** 28 knots **Complement:** 275 **Armament:** 2 x 4.5-inch (single mountings), 2 x 40mm (later replaced by 2 x quad Sea Cat missile launchers), 1 x Mk10 AS Mortar **Aircraft:** Wasp helicopter.

Laid down: 22 October 1959 **Launched:** 19 September 1960

1964	August, returned to Devonport for refit at end of first commission.
1965	Trials and work-up at Portland.
1971	22 November, returned to Devonport, having visited 40 ports in 30 different countries.
1972-73	Refit at Portsmouth. Fitted with Sea Cat guided missiles and improvements to machinery, communications and habitability.
1974	August, deployed to the West Indies, including visits to USA, Bermuda and Caicos Islands.
1975	28 February, gave demonstration of weapon firing and other evolutions to Mexican officials embarked in the Royal Yacht *Britannia* during Her Majesty's State Visit to Mexico. June, in Home Waters.
1975	At the end of the year, she was employed on Fishery Protection duties in the Barents Sea.
1980	March, arrived Chatham to join the Standby Squadron.
1981	August, placed on Disposal list.
1982	17 July, Recommissioned at Devonport having been returned to service to cover for vessels lost and damaged in the Falklands. December, deployed to the West Indies as guardship.
1983	26 June, used explosives to sink 500 ton vessel *Spearfish* that had collided with drilling rig in the English Channel.
1984	29 March, decommissioned at Portsmouth.
1986	3 April, following refit at VT, Woolston, commissioned into Indonesian Navy as *KRI Hasanuddin*.

HMS Tartar (1960)

Her machinery was of a novel design in that it combined steam and gas turbines. The latter's rapid starting properties enabled the ship to leave harbour at short notice; and it boosted the steam turbine when high speed was required.

(Crown Copyright/MoD)

187

HMS Cleopatra (1964)

As completed the Leander class were well proportioned ships. Armament comprised a twin 4.5-inch turret forward, a quadruple Sea Cat launcher on the hangar roof and a Mk10 Limbo AS mortar in a well aft of the small flight deck.

(Crown Copyright/MoD)

CLEOPATRA

Leander Class General Purpose Frigate (Batch 2A)

Displacement: 2,450 tons **Dimensions:** 360 ft x 43 ft x 18 ft **Speed:** 30 knots **Complement:** 262 **Armament:** 2 x 4.5-inch (twin mount), Sea Cat missiles (quad launcher), 2 x 20mm, 1 x Mk10 AS Mortar **Aircraft:** Wasp helicopter

Armament following conversion: 4 x Exocet MM38 missiles, Sea Cat missiles (3 x quad launcher - 1 forward and 2 on hangar roof), 2 x 40mm AA, 6 x ASW Torpedo Tubes (2 x triple mounts) **Aircraft:** Lynx helicopter

Laid down: 19 June 1963 **Launched:** 25 March 1964

1966	1 March, first commissioned for the Far East.
1967	Spent some months with the Portland Squadron as a Training Ship.
1968-69	Far East Station; over Christmas she was employed on the Beira patrol. Returned to Devonport in October, 1969.
1969-70	From November to March she was employed on exercises, trials and training in Home Waters.
1970	May-September, refit at Devonport.
1972	Escort to HM the Queen and HRH the Duke of Edinburgh visiting Singapore.
1973	Carried out patrols in the Cod War off Iceland with *Scylla*.
1973-75	Extensive modernisation at Devonport - the first Leander class frigate to be fitted with the French Exocet anti-ship surface-to-surface guided missile system.
1975	28 November, recommissioned; during trials she deployed to the Bahamas, Florida and Bermuda.
1977	June, attended Silver Jubilee Review of the Fleet.
	September 1977 - April 1978, task Group Six deployment to Far East and Australia with *Tiger*, *Amazon*, *Mohawk*, *Rhyl* and *Dreadnought*, supported by *RFAs Tidepool*, *Grey Rover*, *Regent* and *Tarbatness*.
1978	Refit at Devonport.
1979	April, recommissioned.
1980	September, suffered damage to her deck and starboard side during manoeuvres.
1981	Deployed to the Mediterranean in wake of Russian invasion of Afghanistan.
1982	January, entered refit to receive Type 2031 Towed Array.
1983	June, emerged from refit .
1986	July, New York
	August, Norfolk, Virginia.
1987-89	Major refit at Devonport.
1990	Conducted Exocet missile trials against Goalkeeper off coast of California.
1991	21 August to 11 October, NATO Exercise North Star in North Atlantic.
1992	1 June, decommissioned.
1994	Sold to Cross Seas Shipping Ltd. Beached at Alang, India on 31 January for breaking up.

DANAE

Leander Class General Purpose Frigate

Displacement: 2,450 tons **Dimensions:** 360 ft x 43 ft x 18 ft **Speed:** 28 knots **Complement:** 263 **Armament:** 2 x 4.5-inch (twin mount), Sea Cat missiles (quad launcher), 2 x 20mm, 1 x Mk10 AS Mortar **Aircraft:** Wasp helicopter

Armament following conversion: 4 x Exocet MM38 missiles, Sea Cat missiles (3 x quad launcher - 1 forward and 2 on hangar roof), 2 x 40mm AA, 6 x ASW Torpedo Tubes (2 x triple mounts) **Aircraft:** Lynx helicopter

Laid down: 16 December 1964 **Launched:** 21 October 1965

1967	10 October, first commissioned for trials and work-up at Portland.
1968	19 October, sailed to accompany H.M. the Queen visiting South America.
	After service on Beira patrol, sailed to the Far East.
1970	19 June, recommissioned at Devonport for General Service Commission of four legs - Home/East of Suez/Home/Med.
1972	Toured Eastern Mediterranean and Black Sea.
1974	Persian Gulf and Australia.
1975	November, took part in NATO's largest maritime exercise of the year - 'Ocean Safari' - in N.E. Atlantic and Norwegian Sea.
1976	Further NATO exercises - 'Safe Pass' in March off east coast of USA and 'Open Gate '76' through Straits of Gibraltar.
1977	23 May, returned to Devonport with Seventh Frigate Squadron after 4 months deployment, including a visit to Rio de Janeiro.
1977	1 August, began a 2 year refit at Devonport including installation of Exocet guided missile system.
1980	13 September, recommissioned; her return to sea was delayed by engineering defects to boilers and main engine bearings.
1983	July, emerged from maintenance period with improved close-range armament: a twin 20mm mount fitted aft and two single B-Marc 20mm guns in lieu of ship's boats.
1989	Twelve week docking period extended to fifteen months after serious corrosion found in steel hull plating, frames and longitudinals surrounding the engine and boiler rooms.
1990	Post refit trials followed by five month deployment to the South Atlantic.
1991	July, sold to Ecuador and renamed *Moran Valverde*.

HMS Danae (1965)

HMS Danae was one of seven Leander class to undergo an Exocet conversion. Her 4.5-inch turret has been replaced by four missile canisters for the Exocet anti-ship missile. The Sea Cat capability has been increased by the addition of two further quad launchers and the Limbo mortar removed to provide a larger flightdeck permitting Lynx helicopter operations. Triple ASW torpedo tubes have been added either side of the hangar.

(Syd Goodman Collection)

SCYLLA

Leander Class General Purpose Frigate

Displacement: 2,450 tons **Dimensions:** 360 ft x 43 ft x 18 ft **Speed:** 28 knots **Complement:** 263 **Armament:** 2 x 4.5-inch (twin mount), Sea Cat missiles (quad launcher), 2 x 20mm, 1 x Mk10 AS Mortar **Aircraft:** Wasp helicopter

Armament following conversion: 4 x Exocet MM38 missiles, Sea Wolf missiles (1 x sextuple launcher), 2 x 20mm AA, 6 x ASW Torpedo Tubes (2 x triple mounts) **Aircraft:** Lynx helicopter

Laid down: 17 May 1967 **Launched:** 8 August 1968

1969	16 December, completed for trials.
1970	October-November, off Gibraltar for four weeks of trials - towing the *Penelope* to measure hull noise through the water.
1971	Visited Japan for the annual 'Will Adams Festival' - Adams being credited with the foundation of the Japanese shipbuilding industry.
1972	At Devonport for refit.
1973	22 January, collided with the Torpoint ferry.
	May, in the Cod War off Iceland.
	7 June, deliberately rammed by the Icelandic gunboat *Aegir*, but suffered only superficial damage.
1974	8 March, joint exercise with the U.S.N, and Imperial Iranian Navy in southern Persian Gulf.
	24 June, visited Possession Island, east coast of Australia to commemorate the original ceremony when Lieutenant James Cook landed from *HMS Endeavour* to take possession of the Island 200 years before.
	August, took part in combined exercises off east coast of Malaysia.
1975	1 July, demonstration to Senior Officers and guests of replenishment-at-sea evolutions off Portsmouth.
	4 September, visited Gothenburg, Sweden, when the King of Sweden unveiled a commemorative plaque to the 19th century Admiral, Sir James Saumarez.
1975-76	Further patrols off Iceland in the Cod War.
1976	March, at Devonport presented with the Sopwith Trophy, her ship's flight adjudged the most efficient in 1975.
	25 May, left Plymouth for short spell on Royal escort duties, then to Gibraltar for refit.
1980	August, landed relief parties in the Island of Cayman Brae south of Cuba, which had been devastated by a hurricane.
	November, taken in hand for major refit and conversion for Sea Wolf missile system.
1984	December, completed conversion refit which had been delayed due to manpower being diverted to 1982 Falklands War tasks.
1993	Deployed to South Atlantic.
	December, decommissioned.
2004	27 March, sunk off Whitsand Bay, Cornwall to form an artificial reef; the first of its kind in Europe.

HMS Scylla (1968)

The Sea Wolf conversion required a lot of topweight to be removed from the original ship. The mainmast was replaced by a simple pole mast, the funnel cap was removed and the aft superstructure made much simpler. The Exocet missiles were lowered to the main deck and the port quarter cut away.

(Crown Copyright/MoD)

CRYSTAL

Research and Development Vessel

Displacement: 3,040 tons **Dimensions**: 413 ft 6 in x 56 ft x 5 ft 6 in **Speed:** non-powered **Complement:** 60

Laid Down: 22 June 1970 **Launched:** 22 March 1971

1971	20 March, named. launch delayed by two days due to high winds.
	September, completed.
	30 November, commissioned.
	13 December, towed to Portland.
1975	15 December, towed to Devonport for 6 month refit.
1981	Further refit at Devonport.
1992	18 September, sold to Dutch concern and towed to Rotterdam.

RDV Crystal (1971)

Although not a warship, *RDV Crystal* was the last MoD vessel of significant size to be built and launched at Devonport. She is seen here on her launch day (left) and being manoeuvred in the Hamoaze (above) shortly after entering the water.

(Syd Goodman Collection)

INDEX

A

Aberdeen (1936) 155
Ace (1945) 181
Achates (1945) 181
Adventure (1924) 126
Aeolus (1891) 57
Africa (1862) 7
Algerine (1895) 72
Amethyst (1873) 14
Antelope (1893) 62
Apollo (1934) 153
Arrogant (1896) 75
Astraea (1893) 58
Astrea (1861) 7
Aurora (1913) 108

B

Bideford (1931) 138
Birmingham (1936) 159
Bittern (1861) 8
Bonaventure (1892) 61
Bramble (1938) 167
Britomart (1938) 167
Bulwark (1899) 84

C

Carol (1913) 108
Carron (1867) 9
Centurion (1911) 104, 171
Cleopatra (1915) 114
Cleopatra (1964) 189

Collingwood (1908) 99
Condor (1876) 19
Cornwall (1926) 129
Curlew (1885) 38
Crystal (1970) 195
Cynthia (1861) 8

D

Danae (1965) 190
Devonshire (1927) 130
Dragon (1878) 22
Dryad (1866) 9

E

Edgar (1890) 54
Encounter (1902) 88
Espiegle (1880) 25
Exeter (1929) 133

F

Falmouth (1932) 142
Ferol (1914) 113
Flamingo (1876) 18
Fleetwood (1936) 156
Flirt (1867) 10
Fly (1867) 11
Fowey (1930) 137
Frobisher (1920) 122
Furious (1896) 76

G

Gloucester (1937) 163
Grimsby (1933) 149

H

Halcyon (1894) 66
Harrier (1894) 65
Hastings (1930) 137
Hebe (1936) 160
Hermione (1893) 63
Heroine (1861) 25
Hibernia (1905) 92
Hussar (1894) 69
Hyacinth (1881) 27

I

Icarus (1885) 37
Implacable (1899) 83
Indefatigable (1909) 100

J

J5 (1915) 117
J6 (1915) 117
J7 (1917) 121

K

K6 (1916) 118

K7 (1916) 118
King Edward VII (1903).................................91

L

Landrail (1886) 41
Lapwing (1867)...10
Lapwing (1889)...49
Leander (1931)...141
Leda (1937)...163
Leith (1933) 149
Lion (1910) 103
Londonderry (1935)....................................155
Lowestoft (1934)..150

M

Mariner (1884)...33
Marlborough (1912).....................................107
Milford (1932) 142
Minotaur (1906)...95
Miranda (1879)...23
Modeste (1873)...17
Montagu (1901)...84
Moorfire (1941)...168
Mutine (1880) 23

N

Nassa (1922)
Northumberland (1928) 130

O

Ocean (1863)...8
Ocean (1898)...79
Olna (1921) 125

Orion (1932) 146

P

Partridge (1888) 45
Pegasus (1878)...22
Pelican (1877)...19
Penzance (1930)..134
Perseverance (1875)....................................18
Pheasant (1888)...44
Philomel (1890)...53
Phoebe (1890)...50
Phoenix (1879)...22
Phoenix (1895)...72
Plymouth (1959)..185
Polyphemus (1943)....................................178
Psyche (1898)...80

Q

Queen (1902) 87

R

Racer (1884) 34
Racoon (1887)...42
Rapid (1883)...31
Reindeer (1883) 32
Resistance (1914).......................................114
Ringdove (1889)...50
Royal Oak (1914).......................................113
Royalist (1861) 7
Royalist (1883) 28

S

Salisbury (1953)..182

Sandfly (1887) 42
Sapphire (1874)...17
Scylla (1968)..193
Seagull (1868)...11
Seagull (1937)..164
Serpent (1887)...41
Sharpshooter (1888)......................................46
Sharpshooter (1936)....................................160
Spanker (1889)...47
Speedwell (1889)..49
Spider (1887)...44
Sydney (1948)......................................179,180

T

Talbot (1895)...70
Tartar (1960) 186
Temeraire (1907)...96
Tenedos (1870)...13
Terrible (1944)...178
Thetis (1781)...14
Thule (1942)..173
Totem (1943)..174
Trinidad (1939)..168
Truncheon (1944)..177
Tudor (1942)..173

V

Vigilant (1871)...13

W

Warspite (1913)..110
Watson (1919)..121
Wellington (1934).......................................150
Weston (1932)..145